PATRIARCH KIRILL

In His Own Words

D0912687

St Vladimir's Seminary Press

ORTHODOX CHRISTIAN PROFILES SERIES

Number 7

The Orthodox Christian Profiles Series acquaints the reader on an intimate level with Orthodox figures that have shaped the direction of the Orthodox Church in areas of mission, ascetical and liturgical theology, scholarly and pastoral endeavors, and various other professional disciplines. The people featured in the series are mostly our contemporaries and most remain active in shaping the life of the Church today. A few will have fallen asleep in the Lord, but their influence remains strong and worthy of historical record. The mission of this series is to introduce inspirational Orthodox Christian leaders in various ministries and callings that build up the Body of Christ.

Chad Hatfield
Series Editor

Patriarch Kirill

In His Own Words

ST VLADIMIR'S SEMINARY PRESS

YONKERS, NY 10707

2016

Library of Congress Cataloging-in-Publication Data

CIP Data is on file at the Library of Congress

This book is a joint project of St Vladimir's Orthodox Theological Seminary
and Sts Cyril and Methodius Theological Institute for Post-Graduate Studies
in Moscow. The two sister schools are simultaneously publishing the
Russian original and the English translation of this collection of
Patriarch Kirill's sayings, selected from over three decades of homilies,
speeches, articles, and interviews.

RUSSIAN EDITION, COPYRIGHT © 2016

ENGLISH EDITION, COPYRIGHT © 2016
ST VLADIMIR'S SEMINARY PRESS
575 Scarsdale Rd, Yonkers, NY 10707
1–800–204–2665
www.svspress.com

ISBN 978–0–88141–550–6 (paper)
ISBN 978–0–88141–551–3 (electronic)

PRINTED IN THE UNITED STATES OF AMERICA

Table of Contents

Foreword

By Archpriest Chad Hatfield

This book is intended to introduce an English speaking audience to His Holiness, Patriarch Kirill of Moscow and All-Russia. No contemporary Christian leader has presided over such a remarkable revival of Orthodox Christianity as this patriarch in the post-Soviet era in the Russian Federation. Beginning with the 1000th Anniversary of the Baptism of Rus' in 1988, the Russian Orthodox Church rose up from nearly a century of persecution under the Soviet regime and there was no turning back.

During this time, Patriarch Kirill served as the chairman of the Department for External Relations of the Moscow Patriarchate. Known for his articulate defense of the gospel and diplomatic skills, he was elected patriarch on February 1, 2009. His ministry in the Church has witnessed the end of the Soviet era and an incredible re-building of the spiritual and material elements of Russian Orthodoxy. A great catechetical task was undertaken and overseen by this chief pastor after seventy years of Communist rule came to an end. Cathedrals, churches, monasteries, seminaries and the administration of the largest Orthodox Christian population in the world all needed to be restored. These labors continue even as His Holiness turns seventy years of age.

This is a story that remains largely unknown and unappreciated in the West. Patriarch Kirill is still known through a geopolitical lens that views everything through post-Cold War biases.

This book will allow the reader to meet Patriarch Kirill in his own words, as the title says. The reader will find readings or meditations for every day of the year.

Taken from sermons, addresses, encyclicals and pastoral directives, his deep personal faith in Jesus Christ and his love for Christ's Church shine through these readings, as this bishop, priest, and pastor speaks to his flock in unfiltered words of inspiration. In these pages we discover the spiritual father of a nation in a fresh new light.

This publication comes in thanksgiving for the leadership and voice of Patriarch Kirill. I wish to thank His Eminence, Metropolitan Hilarion of Volokolamsk, Chairman of the Department for External Relations of the Moscow Patriarchate. Andrey Gusev, a graduate of St Vladimir's Seminary and doctoral student in Moscow, worked closely with me in the collection of documents with a team of translators: Fr Christopher Hill, Zinaida Nosova, and Anna Kolesnikova. Ginny Nieuwsma edited the text, and noted how personally rewarding it was to read through the chosen texts. Fr Ignatius Green and the rest of the staff of SVS Press must also be acknowledged for their tireless efforts to bring this new Profile Series book to fruition. Finally, I also want to thank Bronson and Kathleen Eden for their generous support in making this book possible.

Very Rev. Chad Hatfield, D.Min.
C.E.O. of St Vladimir's Orthodox Theological Seminary
St Vladimir's Seminary Press, Profiles Series Editor

Introduction

By Met. Hilarion (Alfeyev)

The present book contains the thoughts of His Holiness Patriarch Kirill, spread over the three hundred and sixty six days of the calendar year, and is the fruit of many years of close cooperation between the Sts Cyril and Methodius Theological Institute for Post-Graduate Studies in Moscow and St Vladimir's Orthodox Theological Seminary in New York.

This book has a definite aim. The voice of the First Hierarch can be heard within Russia and other countries under the canonical jurisdiction of the Russian Orthodox Church, the services he celebrates are broadcast live on central TV stations, his articles and interviews are published in the leading journals and newspapers, and his books are repeatedly published. Yet the American reader has far fewer opportunities to hear the voice of the First Hierarch of the Russian Church without it being distorted through the prism of journalists' views, often politicized and subjective.

This book allows the living voice of Patriarch Kirill to be heard in English for all American readers who want to listen to him. And it is highly significant that it is St Vladimir's Orthodox Theological Seminary that took on the task of publishing this book. In its time the seminary inherited the very best traditions of Russian theology, and its publications today remain one of the main sources that acquaint the American reader with the world of Orthodoxy.

The bulk of the work is made up of carefully selected excerpts from sermons, scholarly articles, presentations, speeches, books and interviews by Patriarch Kirill, covering a period of more than thirty-five years of his pastoral ministry and theological endeavors from 1980 to 2016. On the pages of this book the reader will come to know Patriarch Kirill as a pastor of Christ's Church, as a thinker engaged with contemporary topics, and as a person with deep spiritual experience and a unique gift for preaching.

In one of his interviews, Patriarch Kirill lays stress on the fact that the main purpose of his life is service to God and that at the centre of this service is the celebration of the Divine Liturgy. An important place in this book is also occupied by excerpts from the sermons he has delivered at services. It is precisely these sermons that convey most expressively his living voice, which give a feel for the way his theological ideas flow. In his sermons the patriarch addresses himself to the contemporary human person. He attempts to convey to him in language he can understand the eternal gospel truths, the divine truth which remains unchanged, regardless of the external circumstances of the world. The patriarch reflects on what it means to follow Christ, on serving one's neighbor as the genuine expression of one's faith, and on the transforming power of Christianity.

Yet another important topic for the Patriarch is that of Christian mission. It is natural for a believer to transmit the Good News of salvation which Christ brought, and Patriarch Kirill believes mission work to be the main banner of his ministry.

This book contains resonant quotations from Patriarch Kirill's own mission project, his television program entitled A Pastor's Word, which for more than twenty years has regularly been broadcast on Channel One of Russian state television. Thanks to this program many people, after decades of state atheism, have come to hear about the faith for the first time and have taken their first steps towards God.

The reader of this book will come to know Patriarch Kirill as a thinker in the first instance from the material chosen from his scholarly publications, presentations and speeches dedicated to a common ecclesiastical evaluation of the problems of modern-day society, and the mutual relationship between freedom and responsibility. Patriarch Kirill's labors in this field have made possible the appearance of two very important documents of the Russian Orthodox Church, which have no parallel in the Orthodox world: The Foundations of the Social Concept of the Russian Orthodox Church (2000) and The Foundations of the Teaching of the Russian Orthodox Church on Dignity, Freedom and Human Rights (2008). What ought to be the relationship of the Orthodox Church toward the state and authority? What is the true criterion for genuine creativity? Can the Church recognize freedom without moral responsibility? On the pages of this book the reader will find the answers to these and other questions that concern the faithful throughout the world.

Further important brushstrokes for a portrait of Patriarch Kirill are given by quotations from his autobiographical speeches. He was born and grew up in a country where belief in God was practically forbidden. Nevertheless, even in the conditions of the Soviet school of godlessness, he remained faithful to the truths of Christianity. Courage and lack of compromise when it comes to defending the Orthodox faith are the distinguishing marks of Patriarch Kirill. In this sense he is a worthy successor to the activity of his grandfather Father Vasily Gundyaev, who spent nearly thirty years in prison for his faith, and his teacher Metropolitan Nikodim (Rotov), through whose self-sacrificing labors the Russian Church survived the years of persecution in the 1960s. In this book the reader will find reminiscences of these men, as well as the patriarch's reflections on his own path to God and Church ministry.

The aforementioned topics in no way exhaust the contents of the book, but merely serve to outline its basic ideas. As First Hierarch of the Russian Orthodox Church, Patriarch Kirill is first of all concerned for his Church and flock; he seeks answers to questions relevant to the Russian people. But he is also alarmed by what is happening today in the European Union, America and the Middle East. He touches upon a broad range of topics. However, when opening the book, the reader ought not to forget that at the basis of Patriarch Kirill's varied activities there lies a principle that he considers fundamental: ministry to God and his Church in all things and without reservation. This is the key with which we are to approach this book, so that we do not lose sight of what is important among the myriad of details.

The publishing team that has worked on the book, including colleagues at the Sts Cyril and Methodius Theological Institute for Post-Graduate Studies and St Vladimir's Orthodox Theological Seminary in New York, extend their heartfelt congratulations to His Holiness Patriarch Kirill on the occasion of his seventieth birthday and pray to the Lord that he may preserve him for many blessed years!

†HILARION, Metropolitan of Volokolamsk
Rector of the Saints Cyril and Methodius Theological Institute for Post-Graduate Studies
Chairman of the Synodal Biblical-Theological Commission

General Reflections

Joy and Thanksgiving

1 It is of special importance that, as Orthodox Christians, we are able to rejoice and give thanks to God. Christianity is not a joyless and mournful religion, nor is it a system of taboos that oppresses people and interferes with their lives. Instead, Christianity gives enormous power to people, emancipates their spirits, raises them over their momentary circumstances, and provides them with an immense perspective. . . . And this state of being joyous and thankful to God results from trust in the Lord. Is it not fortuitous that the main sacrament of the Church, the Eucharist, means "thanksgiving" in Greek? We assemble as the Church to give thanks to God because the words "thank you" are the most appropriate ones to say to him.

—*Address at the opening of the International Congress of Orthodox Youth in Moscow* (December 18, 2014)

"We hold dominion over ourselves, and . . . determine the state of our hearts"

2 Love for both our neighbors and those far away brings salvation to the world; this love has no enemies and meets with no obstacles on its way. Even the most rational and just social system cannot make people happy and eliminate all human suffering. Conversely, even the most terrible suffering and imperfection in relationships can be healed by the kindness that is offered from loving hearts. This love requires concrete actions. Whether it becomes reality or not depends on each of us, rather than on the words or actions of politicians. We hold dominion over ourselves, and it is we, and only we, who ultimately determine the state of our hearts.

Today, more than at any other time, attaining personal spiritual perfection is an essential ingredient in fostering universal social values. The heart that is filled with love, compassion, and mercy can break the ice in human relationships, extirpate cruelty, jealousy, and malevolence from these relationships, and fill them with light, blessings, and righteousness. Not only did Christ convey this truth to us in words, but he also made it visible by the very feat of his life.

—*Nativity Message* (January 7, 1991)

"He is open to our prayer and repentance"

3 We must remember that the Lord has not placed cherubim with a flaming sword between himself and us. On the contrary, he is open to our prayer and repentance, and the door to him never closes. He is always near, waiting patiently for us to express our desire and make steps toward him. Adam wished to return to heaven and reconcile with the heavenly Father, but it was impossible. Unlike our forefather fallen into sin, we are able to restore our relationships with God at any moment, for he is always willing to accept our repentance and offer his paternal forgiveness in return.

—*Homily on Cheesefare Sunday* (February 22, 2004)

How to Defeat Pride

4 Many church fathers give us excellent words of advice on how to bring our selfishness under control so that it will not interfere

with our self-understanding and with our efforts to heal our inner sickness.

Contemplating this topic, Symeon the New Theologian suggests that we should be particularly concerned with what happens in us when we are offended, slandered, maligned, or judged unfairly.

In such moments, we cannot hide, brighten up, or neglect to notice the state of our souls, though the glasses through which we view our souls may be murky indeed! This is because we usually react to being offended or slandered with our entire being. Therefore, it is spiritually beneficial for us to analyze this reaction and judge the state of our souls, diagnosing to what extent the disease of selfishness exists within us.

Ultimately, human strength isn't sufficient to win a victory over the self, so the Lord came into this world to win this victory. He became one of us; he united himself with each of us through our shared human nature. Those who become his disciples, follow him, and enter the Church, receive from him the power of his grace, which is sufficient in the hard struggle with the self.

—*Homily on Tuesday of the First Week of Lent* (February 24, 2015)

"Humility is the awareness of the value of other people"

5 Humility is the awareness of the value of other people. The person who places himself at the center of life can never be humble, and this means he cannot accept other people, since he believes them to be lower and weaker than him. All of the calamities that rock human society are based on this perception of the world. Humility is the recognition that all people are God's children, that each has his own talent, his own beauty, and his own spiritual world. The humble person does not trample down the world of his neighbor but instead takes a careful interest in him.

People will always gather around the humble person. When the humble person has a family, he imbues it with spiritual power, love, and mutual respect. The meek person who is humble in heart sees the value of others, and, even if he occupies a position of power, he helps others to manifest their talents without fear of competition. Instead, he places himself in the hands of God and respects the other person.

—*Homily on the feast of St Sergius of Radonezh* (October 8, 2010)

The meaning and purpose of human life

6 The biblical story of creation shows that God made the world unfinished and designed man to work and keep it (Gen 2.15) and thus to participate with him, the Creator, in perfecting and completing the creation. In other words, man is called not only to pursue his own personal perfection, but also to perfect the world around him and to become a co-worker of God. The infinite perfection of the human person and our participation in perfecting creation through our cooperation with God are truths so lofty and great that they seem to be remote from today's problems. And yet it is these truths that make up, by the will of God, the meaning and purpose of human life. You must be perfect, as your heavenly Father is perfect (Mt 5.48), as the gospel says.

—*Nativity Message* (January 7, 1997)

Chastity: The Foundation for All Growth

7 What does God create us for? He intends us to live with inner integrity. We can only achieve this by separating the good from the evil, so that good may fill our hearts and conquer our minds, so that we may throw off all evil and deception. The Church calls the inner integrity of the person "chastity,"[1] a virtue that is the foundation for all true intellectual, moral, and spiritual growth.

What is true for the individual is equally true for both family and society. Maintaining the unity of the family is impossible unless husband and wife remain chaste. If, in family life, truth is mixed up with falsehood and good adjoins evil, such a family will not stand the test of time, because it loses its chastity as well as its inner integrity. According to the gospel, if a house is divided against itself, that house will not able to stand (Mk 3.25).

—*Nativity Message* (January 7, 2008)

Morality and Freedom

8 Once human rights and freedoms were elevated above all other values and moral standards, religion was forced from the public sphere, and the decline of moral standards and traditional morality was the consequence. Human rights and freedoms remain valuable and constructive as long as they are understood in the context of moral responsibility and religious teaching. If morality becomes relative, however, "freedom" begins to be understood as a total absence of authority. Only within a framework of morality can we restrain and direct free choice toward the good. Freedom ought not to be considered in isolation from our responsibility to God, to others, to ourselves, and to the voice of our conscience. Likewise, rights do not exist without duties, including those moral ones issuing from the moral nature of man.

—*Speech when receiving the doctor* honoris causa *at the University of Belgrade* (November 14, 2014)

---

[1]The root meaning of the Greek word for "chastity"—*sōphrosynē*—is "whole-minded." This points to a state of inner integrity and wholeness, not merely outward sexual continence.—*Ed.*

How to Conquer Despondency

9 Strong faith and trust in the Lord turn any kind of despondency to ashes. When the moment of despondency comes, say these simple words to the Lord: "Thy will be done in everything! In grief, which thou dost send over me; in sorrow or in bodily and spiritual weakness; thou, O Lord, allowed these things to happen. Help me get out of this state by thy power."

Then turn to the Lord with fervent prayer from the heart. God is never mocked (Gal 6.7). The answer to this prayer is that the man who earlier knelt down, being overcome with despondency and grief, will rise up transformed. Sometimes it takes a while. But one should not lose one's faith in firmly believing that everything is in the hands of God—life and death, happiness and grief. When we commit ourselves into the hands of God, we become capable of shaking off the drowsiness born from despondency, and we find we have renewed energy for self-improvement and tackling the problems that contributed to our despondency.

—*Homily on Wednesday of the First Week of Lent*
(February 25, 2015)

Theological Studies and Spiritual Preparation

10 The study of theology is a magnificent undertaking when it arises, first of all, out of inner spiritual experience through a life of prayer, rather than out of mere logic and knowledge. If a theologian becomes simply an armchair scholar with head knowledge and debating skills, then that person is in danger of succumbing to false teaching. However, if the scholar lives an intense spiritual life; if the divine liturgy is life itself rather than simply a solemn ceremonial occasion to go to church on festal days; if prayer is his daily necessity, and repentance and self-examination are his daily practices—then such an intellectual will never say a word against the truth of God. Instead, his knowledge, coupled with his spiritual experience, will result in tremendous thought and spiritual force, which was the case for the holy fathers.

One cannot approach the divine things without being spiritually prepared. Our theological study should bring us closer to God and help us grasp the mystery of God. Divine mysteries will be revealed only in the depth of the heart that is committed to the Lord and living in obedience and simplicity.

—*Homily on the First Sunday of Lent* (March 1, 2015)

"We are called . . . to keep and perfect the world"

11 By building our lives on the foundation of the divine law and the power of the divine grace within the Church, Christians can overcome evil and untruth both within ourselves and within the world around us. We can create eternal and imperishable values: good, love, peace, and justice. As we embody these values, we raise others aloft, making life more illuminated and joyful. Since we are called not only to strive for personal perfection but also to keep and perfect the world, we must apprehend all that is going on around us, furthering everything that increases good and stops evil.

—*Nativity Message* (January 7, 1997)

How Can We Overcome Divisions?

12 The Church proclaims her word and carries out her mission in the world. How many walls of separation, similar to those that divided the Gentiles and the Jews (cf. Eph 2.14), exist in this world! It is impossible even to list the types of divisions among men: social, cultural, linguistic, spiritual. Men are divided by various political convictions and ideals, and they are split by their economic status into rich and poor. Yet we invite the whole divided world to enter the Church and therefore put an end to the divisions.

How can this change be possible? What if it is mere fantasy? What if the Church is unable to preach the truth that overcomes all the barriers among men? May it never be so! The word of God and the record of the Church's life testify that all this is possible: I can do all things through Christ who strengthens me (Phil 4.13).

What has to be done for men to become united in community in spite of all the differences among them? People must hear the tidings of Christ rather than a repetition of formulas from past centuries. We must preach such a word that can help our hearers to grasp in an instant that in Christ not only are all obstacles overcome, but abundant life is granted!

—*Homily on the Twenty-Fourth Sunday after Pentecost*
(November 23, 2014)

"Forgiving one another, even as God in Christ forgave you" (Eph 4.32)

13 The Lord can save any sinner, even one whom society refuses to forgive. The Lord can save the criminals that society isolates. We know of cases where prisoners, after being released, changed their lives so radically that they became examples for others. The power of God extends to all men, for, as he says, he sends rain on the just and the unjust and makes the sun rise on the evil and the good (cf. Mt 5.45).

The saints show their power by helping sinners see the mercy and love of God, which all too often we fail to manifest. We can talk about love, but when the time comes to make an effort to help the downtrodden, we make excuses. "Does this man even deserve to converse with us and receive our help, much less receive our sympathy for his grief?" ... We ought to forgive sinners rather than condemn them. Without showing partiality, we ought to be able to do good things, not only to those who do so to us and who appear to be righteous in our eyes, but also to those who appear to be unrighteous. This fulfills Christ's commandment to love our neighbors. Through our love for others, we in turn will enter that divine life which doesn't end with earthly life but expands into eternity.

—*Homily on the feast of St Matrona of Moscow* (May 2, 2014)

"Faith demands our full involvement"

14 The Lord did not say that to have life in him, one needs to perform deeds of renown, such as building magnificent structures, achieving scientific breakthroughs, offering profound insights in the realm of thought, or producing excellent works of art. Nor did he say that one needs to have power over men and use it for good, or that in order to enjoy his life a man or woman must be strong, rich, and prosperous. The only thing he said is this: everyone who believes Jesus is the Christ, the Savior and the Son of God, will have life in him. Therefore, faith is the power that can bring us into eternity; no other power nor virtue nor any other human dimension of our lives suffices for us to reach eternity in God, because it is only faith that matters. ...

But why did it please God to have faith determine human salvation, to make salvation entirely dependent on our faith? The reason is that faith demands our full involvement. Everyone who has prayed fervently at least once in his life, for example, out of fear of death for oneself or a loved one, knows what true prayer is. Praying in Gethsemane, Christ sweat blood. One can imagine how fierce his struggle must have been when he was praying so fervently! Faith demands such concentration; that is why it is a necessary condition for our salvation.

—*Homily on the Second Sunday after Pascha* (April 27, 2014)

"*Through the cross, joy has entered the world!*"

15 The Savior's life, his sufferings on the cross, his painful death on Golgotha, and his resurrection pose the most convincing reason for Christians to trust and be confident in divine providence, which leads us through life's various troubles. Indeed, had the Lord Jesus Christ not endured Golgotha in his earthly life, or had the incarnate Word of God come into the world for the careless, happy, and joyous dwelling in it, then the troubles befalling us would seem unbearable and could shake our faith. The Lord chose the way of suffering for the sins of man and the way of the saving cross. Our God was pleased to drink the cup of human sufferings to the dregs, overcoming adverse and compelling circumstances, struggling to the last gasp, enduring reproach, mocking, death agonies, and finally death itself. "Through the cross, joy has entered the world!"[2]

Whenever the circumstances of life push us toward the precipice of despondency and despair, or whenever we see no reasonable explanation for our setbacks and miseries, we must not lose heart. On the contrary, our faith must grow even stronger. We must say to ourselves: God, who knows what we need better than we, offers us this way of life, and not the other, so it is this way that we ought to go with patience and hope. A faithful person has the means to conquer despondency and cope with despair, for he knows the words of St Paul, "We are hard-pressed on every side, yet not crushed; we are perplexed, but not in despair; persecuted, but not forsaken; struck down, but not destroyed—

---

[2]From the hymn "Having beheld the resurrection of Christ . . ." (sung after the gospel at Sunday matins).

always carrying about in the body the dying of the Lord Jesus, that the life of Jesus also might be manifested in our body" (2 Cor 4.8–10).

—*Homily on Monday of the First Week of Lent* (February 26, 2001)

"By your patience possess your souls" (Lk 21.19)

16 Patience, as well as humility and meekness, reveals not the weakness but the strength of a man. This strength is not illusory and outward; rather, it is real and deep, bringing great happiness and contentment. When we possess patience, we guard our innermost life and mental world against the evil and soul-destroying effects of physical illness or spiritual sorrow. Often our innermost world suffers when others purposefully strive to influence us, attempt to shatter our spiritual strength, and try hard to change the state of our souls to their own advantage.

The believer's weapon in this battle ought to be the tranquility of his interior life. Then insults will not rouse feelings of animosity in our souls, or the urgent desire to take revenge on the offender. Remember well this rule: any evil aimed at a man only succeeds if it rouses reciprocal evil in his soul.

—*Homily on Tuesday of the First Week of Lent* (February 27, 2001)

The Law of Harmony

17 It was pleasing to God to build the whole universe upon the law of harmony. Harmony unites even diverse elements to make of them a single whole, which is marked with divine beauty. When harmony is violated, then evil conquers good. That is why the great Russian writer Dostoevsky said, "Beauty will save the world." He was not referring to the beauty of human faces or clothing, but to the divine law of harmony that saves the world by manifesting a particular visible aspect of the divine beauty.

—*Homily on the feast of the icon of the Mother of God,*
  "Life-Giving Spring" (April 17, 2015)

"Whoever loses his life for my sake will find it" (Mt 16.25)

18 When approaching the end of his life, a man who has lived only for himself quite often understands that he has nothing but emptiness inside him. He might start to think: if only I could start everything from the very outset! But the Lord thus says to us all: a man must choose to lose his life for the sake of Christ and the gospel in order to not have such gloomy thoughts at the end of his life.

What is required of us? We must place the Lord at the center of our lives and direct our spiritual energies toward choosing the salvific path of living for others. The Lord does not suggest each of us should become an ascetic or hermit or monk. He does not suggest we should seek suffering. He simply suggests that we dedicate our lives to fulfilling his law, his commandments, and the gospel. In this case, we will retain all we possess, all the fortune we earned.

—*Homily on the Third Sunday of Lent*
  (March 15, 2015)

"He . . . sends rain on the just and on the unjust" (Mt 5.45)

19 The Lord grants inspiration unto different men, even those who are not faithful and pious. Why so? The reason is that the love of God extends to all men. Rain and sunshine are sent on the just and unjust (cf. Mt 5.45). The great mercy of God is shown in this. If it were not the case, then the Church would become an elite group of inspired men, which would inevitably cause another division among people between those who were "inspired" and those lacking divine grace. But the Lord is the Father of all. He gives his gifts to all, and it is up to us whether to accept these gifts or not.

—*Homily on the Fifth Sunday after Pascha* (May 10, 2015)

"This synthesis of knowledge, faith, and living piety"

20 If a pastor's word is torn away from theology it is dangerous. If a pastor's word is torn away from reality it is irrelevant; it is of no interest to anybody. Therefore, the task is that we—basing ourselves on the sources of our faith and without subjecting these sources to revision in our consciousness—should find the right words in order to teach people in writing and by word of mouth to form the outlook of the modern Orthodox man. In a few words, it is the great task that faces our theology. And to do it, future workers in this field should be theologically educated, they should be well-versed in languages, both old and new, and they should read modern literature while preserving the power of our spiritual tradition. They should necessarily be people of prayer; otherwise theology is not for them. A theologian who does not pray is not a theologian. A theologian who has no living relation with God is not a theologian. To be effective one should form in oneself this synthesis of knowledge, faith, and living piety.

—*Speech to the students of the Sts Cyril and Methodius Theological Institute for Post-Graduate Studies* (November 1, 2015)

True Freedom and the Image of God

21 My reflections on human freedom can be summarized thus: in itself, freedom is a great gift of God and affords us the ability to choose. God did not program us to do good deeds; we must choose to do them.

People often ask, "Why does God not punish the sinners? Where is God when such things as wars and crimes take place?" God has not programmed us to do good things in the way we set our alarms to wake us up at a certain hour. Of course, he could have done this. He could have created a wonderful community composed of happy and holy people. But then these people would have been holy and happy not by their own free wills, but because they were programmed to be this way. Without true freedom, we would not carry the image of God within us. In his will, God created us in his own image and put in us the breath of his life. By doing so, he bequeathed to us the ability to choose.

—*Address at Yerevan State University* (March 18, 2010)

The Disease of Pride

22 A man who is subject to pride becomes weak and vulnerable. It might seem to him that he is strong, since pride most often makes inroads into the souls of clever, educated, and lucky men. But by driving God from his life and putting himself in God's place, such a man becomes very vulnerable. Pride shows us the true face of sin, with its ugliness and abnormality. We were created to fulfill God's law, obey God's commandments, and live in accordance with them. This is the norm of human life set by God! The holy fathers explain that when pride takes over a man's heart, distortions and abnormalities occur in the soul, which then becomes spiritually diseased.

—*Homily on Wednesday of the First Week of Lent* (March 20, 2013)

Setting our Spiritual Priorities

23 One ought to set priorities in the right order; spiritual life is no hobby or entertainment for which we may or may not have enough time. Spiritual life is the basis upon which we build up all the rest. When you are packing your luggage in the suitcase, whether your belongings can fit in the suitcase or not depends not only on the size or number of your items, but also on the order and sequence in which you pack them. When we live our lives in vain pursuits, we are tossed to and fro, we have no time for anything eternal or spiritual, and we feel tired all the time.

If we begin our day with prayer we will form the basis upon which all can be built up in the right order. The Scripture once said about a pious man, "Whatever he does shall prosper" (Ps 1.3).

—*"Patriarch Kirill: Spiritual life is no hobby for which we may or may not have enough time," interview with the magazine* Foma (May 6, 2013)

False Freedom Destroys Us

24 Today both Catholic and Orthodox Christians are facing the same tasks, challenges, and problems that ought to be resolved within the Christian tradition.

We see what is going on in the so-called consumer society, in which moral taboos are annihilated. In fact, the very project of taboo annihilation is seen as a positive thing: what could be better than to set man completely free! Yet we are aware that man is not a sinless creature, so when setting him entirely "free," we also let out this dark, Dionysian (as the Greeks called it) impulse. We emancipate instincts, but then try to put this "emancipated" person in order by enacting laws.

We shed crocodile tears over corruption or crimes. Yet corruption and crimes are an outcome of sin, and no machinery of law can ever conquer sin! Now we see where this is leading us today: the "emancipated" society fails to restrain human vices and finally gives up on all such attempts at restraint. Do whatever you like! Moreover, vices have even become legalized and justified by laws.

All this eventually destroys the human person. Today, we see unfolding before us a mounting crisis that alternately arises in the economy, finances, ecology, and politics. The world is in confusion. The source of this confusion, however, is not in the events we learn about in the daily TV news, but in man himself as a human person. This is the main challenge for followers of the Christian tradition, for the churches of West and East—for the Orthodox and Catholic churches.

—*Interview on Pascha for the TV channel* Russia-1 (May 5, 2013)

The "absolute criterion for the genuineness of our relationship with God"

25 Christ the Savior has established an unshakeable, absolute criterion for the genuineness of our relationship with God, and that criterion is how we love our neighbor. In taking upon ourselves others' infirmities, sharing their pain and afflictions, and in being compassionate to the unfortunate and downtrodden, we fulfill the law of Christ (cf. Gal 6.2) and are likened to the Savior, who took upon himself our infirmities and carried our illnesses (cf. Is 53.4).

It is impossible on this joyful and light-bearing day of Christ's nativity, when all of creation falls down in amazement before the crib of the divine infant, to forget about others. The abundant grace that we receive today in our churches is to be poured out upon those who are still beyond the confines of the Church and who live according to the elements of this world and not according to Christ (Col 2.8). If we do not go together to greet them, then this good news of the Savior may not reach them; if together we do not open up our hearts in order to share the joy which has filled us, then it may never touch those who do not yet have it, but who are ready to receive it.

—*Nativity Message* (January 7, 2014)

"Monastics influence the world by the power of their prayer"

26 It is the saints who exert decisive influence on what is going on in the human heart. In some sense, saints influence the march of history. Textbooks do not write about it. They feature heads of state, military commanders, revolutions and other events, but nothing is said, for instance, about how the example of a saint can change people's lives. This example is given us by the Mother of God: God vouchsafed to the most holy virgin his special grace, and she changed the life of the world in such a way as none of even the greatest state or political leaders did. And if we understand the immutable truth that one's spiritual life is important not only for oneself, it becomes clear: even the most secluded monastic life, in which and through which a spiritual feat is performed, can influence the surrounding world, and the examples of saints clearly show it. Sometimes we are told: "Why should monks be reclusive? Rather, they should address the world and influence the world!" Of course, they should, and the Church's pastoral word is addressed to the world, but monastics influence the world by the power of their prayer and spiritual accomplishment, and once having come in touch with it, many change their attitude to God, to the Church, and very often, to their whole life.

—*Address to the Meeting of Abbots and Abbesses of the Russian Orthodox Church* (September 23, 2016)

"Without doing good, man cannot live"

27 In our lives, we ought always to do as much good as we possibly can. For Christ did not call on us to perform extraordinary deeds. He called on us simply to feed those in need of food and to visit the ill and imprisoned. These are such simple things to do. If we learn to be good to each other, starting with our private lives and families, we will be changing for the better.

We ought to be accustomed to doing good deeds. A man without this habit is a deficient person. To not know how to do the good and right thing is more dangerous than not having a university degree or professional skills. A man without good is no longer a human being, and a culture made up of people like this creates a wolf pack, as we can now see from reading about today's criminals. Let us all, then, learn to do good, beginning on a small scale. Everyone who has chosen this way will soon understand that this is of vital importance; without doing good, man cannot live.

—*Interview on the TV channel* Russia-24 (January 7, 2012)

God's Love

28 Love is God's miracle, not a selective gift given to an elite few. This gift is not the same as the talents God gives us that allow us to be musicians, mathematicians, or physicians. Love is available to all, even as the air is. Yet how we accept this gift from God depends on each particular person. One person receives so much exposure to the sun that he is then brought to the hospital, while another finds that the bright rays of sunshine improve his health.

This is also how it is with love. Love is a wonderful gift of God that we can accept or reject. If we receive this love with open arms, we will find ourselves united with all men. Other things such as our talents or our ethnic, cultural, and political differences lead to divisions. Only love is capable of uniting people.

—*Interview on the TV channel* Russia-1, *on the eve of the first anniversary of the Patriarchal Enthronement* (January 31, 2010)

We Must Choose Love

29 Love is God's gift, but we are the ones who respond to this gift. Whether we love or not depends on our human will toward the good. Here is a simple example. You hold a poor opinion about a certain person; you dislike him for his appearance or his nature. Indeed, we know there are many things that alienate one person from another. You can then give in to this feeling and nurse it, or you can try to overcome this feeling. One way to overcome this is to make an effort to change your opinion about the man into a good one. Another method is to do good to this man. When we do good things for people, they remain in our hearts forever.

Among other things, love is thus an orientation of the human will in which we choose deeds of kindness toward others. Falling in love as two teenagers do produces a happy, light feeling. Yet life will show them whether deep, abiding love is present or not. To progress from falling in love to growing in love, one must direct one's will to the good, share one's life with the other, and give up a part of one's self to the other.

—*Interview on the first anniversary of the Enthronement* (January 31, 2010)

The Church and the World

30 One should not expect or demand that the Church lead the masses by encouraging the attainment of earthly goals. In this, the Church would merely be following the ideological, philosophical, and common orientation of people. The Church's task is to call all to salvation to the extent that they desire this salvation and are able to respond to it. In the coming of his Son our Lord Jesus Christ, God revealed and is still revealing himself to this world, but the Lord draws no one to himself by force. Every man, glimpsing the image of the incarnate God in Christ, understands that only this Man, this power, and these thoughts can save the world.

—*"A Pastor's Word," the patriarch's TV program* (May 11, 2013)

Values that Unite

31 Society can be united only on the basis of values that transcend the changing opinions and fads of the day. Justice and truth have always been such transcendent values, rooted in an absolute God. God doesn't change his opinions and attitudes depending on popular opinion; he is the absolute and unchanging God. His law is the fixed value system that informs all other value systems relevant to human existence. If you destroy this absolute value, then everyone lives in whatever way he likes, relying on his own understanding of good and evil.

—*"A Pastor's Word," the patriarch's TV program*
  (December 13, 2014)

The True Nature of Justice

32 No one, even at the United Nations, raises the question of the true nature of justice. All know for certain the meaning that justice has in international relations and other spheres of human life. And when laws are enacted that destroy or challenge justice— whether it be fascist or racist laws or any other such laws—the global community rises against them, because these laws conflict with a universally recognized concept of justice.

Therefore, if justice is the same for all, then the source of such justice cannot be rooted in any group of men whose tastes and preferences are inevitably influenced by the current epoch in which they live, their place of residence, the surrounding culture, and many other variables. No, we all can acknowledge a certain common justice. The whole system of law is associated with this justice. Scholarship even has a particular section called "Law and Morality." Once separated from morality, law becomes unjust.

So, what morality guarantees justice for all humanity, regardless of place or time? Only that moral impulse that originates in the absolute principle and greatest absolute value—that is, God—can do this. Therefore, whenever we speak about justice, we are using religious language.

—*"A Pastor's Word," the patriarch's TV program*
(December 13, 2014)

The Importance of the Liturgy

33 In my time, when I was still a theological student, I received an exhortation from my spiritual father, His Eminence Metropolitan Nikodim (Rotov), which has remained important for me throughout my life. With his blessing I had to undertake accelerated training in the academy; the load was heavy and, preparing for another exam, I failed to attend the service for the Dormition of the most holy Mother of God. The next day His Eminence asked me, "Why were you not present at the service?" I said, "Vladyka, an exam was imminent, and there was a vast amount of material. I simply could not make it." And he said the words I have remembered all my life: "You will never make it and you will never achieve anything if you do your tasks at the expense of the liturgy." So I try to stick to his words as much as I can,

though I do not always manage to do it, because of my weakness. I am deeply convinced that for a bishop, a monk, and for a parish priest as well, the celebration of the liturgy is the most important task because it is the liturgy that raises us beyond the everyday, arming us with spiritual power and helping us to have the right view of the everyday problems we encounter in fulfilling our duties—administrative, economic, and others.

—*Address to the Meeting of Abbots and Abbesses of the Russian Orthodox Church* (September 23, 2016)

"Good is greater than evil"

34 Had the number of bad events been greater than that of good ones, human history would have come to an end, because evil destroys good and in itself lacks vitality and life. A civilization built on evil will not exist indefinitely, because evil is death and non-existence. Though we live in a world in which there is too much grief and we often are staggered by its injustice, we must remember that even in such a world, by God's mercy good is greater than evil.

Good may not be so striking or sensational, however. One of the tendencies within modern journalism is, unfortunately, to publicize negative incidents, because bad news attracts more attention. Indeed, I know of many members of the press who quickly skip over any positive news in order to focus their attention on negative stories. If we hear only bad news and our attention is focused exclusively on that, the result is that we will begin to view our days, weeks, and even our entire epoch in an exclusively negative manner. In reality, this is not the way we should perceive our circumstances, because by God's mercy, good prevails over evil.

—*"A Pastor's Word," the patriarch's TV program* (October 11, 2014)

"For now we see in a mirror, dimly, but then face to face" (1 Cor 13.12)

35 There can be nothing worse than forming judgments regarding matters that are hidden from us. Perhaps we are critical when a criminal, a cruel person, or even an atheist unexpectedly confesses and receives holy communion. Yet do we really think such events happen by accident? Perhaps this deathbed confession and participation in the anointing of the sick crowned his life! Perhaps he was on the journey toward this event from the time of his birth, and the Lord made him worthy of this grace at the brink of death. On the other hand, the Lord might allow a just man who regularly confessed and received the Eucharist to repose without confession and the Eucharist, since such a man was already worthy of crossing the divide between his life and eternal life.

While we can guess the answers to these questions, we will only know them with certainty when we approach the end of our lives. The Apostle Paul said that now we see this divine reality as through a dim mirror (cf. 1 Cor 13.12). We see only patches of light and cannot fully glimpse what lies beyond; when we die, we will see all things face to face.

—*"A Pastor's Word," the patriarch's TV program* (June 12, 2014)

The Church Militant

36 Many critics make the greatest mistake when they look in from outside the Church and notice imperfections, and fiercely criticize not only the Church, but also the faith itself on the grounds of their observations. Unto the end of the age, the Church militant, as the holy fathers called it—struggling against sin—will be running the Church's ministry. This ministry will never be easy and comfortable work; it will always be accompanied by struggle.

All the clergy and laity of the past, present, and future will be involved in this great work of the salvation of human souls.

Also, it is important and desirable that those looking from the outside realize they are also involved in this great struggle, and that they come as soon as possible to the Church. Thus they will change their positions from that of outside observers to that of participants in the great work of the spiritual salvation of the human race. That work is carried out by the divine power in the Church and through the Church.

—*"A Pastor's Word," the patriarch's TV program* (June 10, 2012)

We Are Free to Choose

37 Freedom is at the heart of man's turning to God and at the heart of man's communion with God. For the Lord could have compelled us to go to church, believe in him, and do what he teaches. But the Lord does not rule over our will in such a manner! He leaves the ability to choose up to us. You come to church, listen to what is said there, watch what is going on there, and unburden your soul as the ministry of the Church positively affects your soul. No one has the right to enslave your conscience; no one has the right to direct your activity or force his will on you—you make your choice on your own.

—*"A Pastor's Word," the patriarch's TV program* (April 7, 2012)

Modern Distractions and the Importance of Fasting

38 We live in a world that we cannot escape. Information flows into our homes and into our bedrooms. Many people have a television set right next to the bed! With this constant barrage, man opens his mind to all the trends of this age. A more careful look at what the modern world offers to a fasting person points to a sorrowful conclusion: all of this constitutes an overwhelming temptation for the mind, feelings, and will. Never has man had such temptations, such lures. These temptations don't strike with frontal assault, but gradually enter the consciousness, subtly forming a negative attitude toward Christian values. . . .

Fasting is far harder today, yet the fruit of fasting is far more important and needed today as well. A man who can overcome the evil attractions brought to bear by all the distractions of our modern technological civilization becomes truly free and hears the call of the Lord. He finds communion with him and, consequently, fullness of life and life eternal.

— *"A Pastor's Word," the patriarch's TV program* (April 7, 2012)

Preserving Our Marriages and Our Marriages Preserving Us

39 Marriage ends with the end of love, and so the cause of family break-ups lies in what can be called a crisis of love. Such things also happened in the past, but then people were trained differently—they had the fear of God in their hearts. Even if something happened in their hearts and their mutual feelings changed, prayer to God and good deeds preserved family relations and marriage.

There was a time when people would endure troubles and then at a mature age come to understand that the preservation of their marriage was the greatest value of their lives. Only that steadfast relationship could save them from the cold winds coming from the outside. For these people, marriage remained a real home, a castle, and a place where people supported each other—honestly, disinterestedly, and under the most difficult circumstances.

— *"A Pastor's Word," the patriarch's TV program* (February 11, 2012)

Modern Disorientation and the Criterion of Truth

40 Any person may have doubts as to what concerns life and the values of this life. A more careful look at the crises arising in modern society will reveal that all of them are somehow related to the loss of orientation. People have a lot of knowledge, but are nevertheless disoriented. They have many ideas, but no criterion or standard to judge what is true. There are as many opinions as there are men. This situation results in a very particular state for people. If "there are as many opinions as there are men," then under the triumph of freedom and human rights, everyone has the ability and right not only to publicly present his own wisdom, but also to lead other men. . . .

We will never lose our way, however, if we live in the light of God's divine wisdom. In this light, even if we lose the way, we will find it again. Divine wisdom will illumine our way because it is the criterion of truth. Reject anything that conflicts with the word of God, and live in accordance with this word. This is the only true way in your life.

—*"A Pastor's Word," the patriarch's TV program*
(January 8, 2012)

The Alternative to the "Civilization of Instinct"

41 The creation of a "civilization of instinct" poses the most dangerous threat to humanity. Human demands, passions, and cravings are stimulated in order to encourage the acquisition of wealth and material things, which in turn develop the economy. The outcome of this developed economy is that it offers further encouragement to the vicious circle of instinct and desire in which men continue to create, by their work, a civilization of instinct.

One can say, "What shall we do? A man cannot live without it! We seem to have been predestined to improve our knowledge and technology in order to perfect the world." Yes, it is absolutely true. But this knowledge can only be handled correctly when it is counterpoised by a strong moral sense and the voice of conscience, the latter being the ability to live in accordance with the law of God.

—*"A Pastor's Word," the patriarch's TV program* (January 9, 2011)

Deny Yourself and Take Up Your Cross

42 How often we are surprised by our circumstances! We grow indignant and sometimes begin to complain to God, saying, "What evil have I done that such a misfortune befell me?"

Though such a thought comes to our minds, the Lord doesn't remove our cross. To save our souls, to achieve fullness of life and inner peace, to balance our inner forces, and even to become successful in life as we grow through struggle, a mandatory first step is that we learn to bear the cross that God gives us!

We may begin to throw down our cross in anger, and blame our misfortune on the entire world, or on our relatives and friends. In reality, they have nothing to do with it, but are only an easy target for us as we work off our emotions. Indeed, we will never succeed by venting and complaining at those in authority over us. But if we do not get angry or irritated and do not complain to God, but instead commit ourselves into the hands of God and accept and bear the cross, then we take the first step toward growing rich in God. In this way, our souls will not perish, and we will find salvation by accepting Christ and his commandments.

—*Homily on the Third Sunday of Lent* (March 15, 2015)

The Mission of the Church in Each Generation

43 The Christian Church focuses its close attention, first of all, on the care of the human soul. It is the priests' duty to inculcate in people the ability and means of self-improvement and the elevation of their spirits. The Church's duty is to preserve the values coming from God himself, rather than to load men with burdens hard to bear. There is nothing more important than these values. God revealed to men how they must live and what they must do in order to attain salvation. And this news, proclaimed by the Savior, is preserved in the Church.

The Church supplements and enhances this word of God with wonderful commentary from the holy fathers and through the decisions of the ecumenical and local councils. She interprets the word of God with regard to each particular epoch, enlivening and updating that word for each new generation. This is what the mission of the Church is about.

—*"A Pastor's Word," the patriarch's TV program* (February 12, 2011)

"A healthy balance between ethnic and universal loyalties"

44 Patriotism is a natural and vital feeling, without which neither states nor ethnic communities can function. Patriotism helps people feel that they are one ethnic group and one nation. But patriotism, improperly understood, can result in dangerous interpretations and implications. Patriotism, if it is not counterpoised by Christian and religious morality, can easily grow into aggressive nationalism. In the Church, however, our Christian morality allows us to maintain a healthy balance between ethnic and universal loyalties. That is why patriotism in the Church never poses any danger to others; the patriotism of a faithful man poses no danger to others.

—*"A Pastor's Word," the patriarch's TV program* (March 6, 2011)

How People Find Their Way to the Church

45 Due to the nature of my job and my ministry, I have often had to read autobiographies of men applying for studies at theological schools, going to monasteries, or asking for a blessing to become a monk or to take holy orders. In their autobiographies, these people often write about their spiritual journeys rather than simply limiting themselves to listing previous studies or occupations. Instead, they often share how they found their way to the Church, and in this respect, one thing has repeatedly drawn my attention.

At a mature age, people most often come to faith through communicating with their friends and colleagues. Eventually they will come to church and listen, but frequently it is in those initial talks with friends, neighbors, or colleagues where they begin to develop a nascent belief in God and begin to turn their minds to God. When a faithful person is able to tell an inquirer about his own religious experience and faith, these conversations most often become the first spark that sets the religious feeling in a man on fire.

—*"A Pastor's Word," the patriarch's TV program* (May 28, 2011)

"The fear of the Lord is the beginning of wisdom" (Prov 9.10)

46 Living with God means that we always rely on his divine power. Sin ruins this reliance, and thus we become lonely, with all the consequences that ensue, both for our earthly life and for the life to come. For this reason, wise people are afraid to break God's commandments. This fear causes no terror, nor does it paralyze people's consciousness. Instead, it helps direct their lives in accordance with God's law and God's truth, enabling them to hold fast to this truth, whatever temptations, seductions, and human infirmities might try to lead them away from it.

—*"A Pastor's Word," the patriarch's TV program* (May 28, 2011)

"He who is faithful in what is least is faithful also in much" (Lk 16.10)

47 During a fast we restrict ourselves, curbing our wishes. Truly we train our will, becoming stronger and scoring a victory over ourselves. How else can we achieve changes if we do not win a victory over ourselves? If we fail in such a small thing as food restriction, what can be said about bigger things? What tasks, which require self-restriction, can one set oneself if even the smallest thing has proved impossible? Therefore, fasting as self-restriction in food is a very important indicator of one's willingness and ability to achieve one's inner spiritual growth.

There is, however, another very important thing related to fasting. We fast because there is the church statute. By restricting ourselves, we impose on ourselves certain spiritual fetters. What do we do it for? We do it because of our obedience to the Lord. It is our small sacrifice to God, small but essential. And the Lord sees our wish to assume the burden for his sake, for the fulfillment of his commandments, for being closer to him, for changing our mind and heart. This feat of fasting comes up to the Lord as a fragrant sacrifice, and the Lord responds to us (because he is never indebted to us). If we forgo our interests and restrict ourselves for his sake, the Lord makes up for this limitation, as it were, by that which is more essential for man—by a change in our inner state, a change of our mind and heart.

—*Homily on Monday of the First Week of Lent* (March 18, 2013)

Man's Dignity in a God-fearing Society

48 Man holds a place of exclusive dignity and is elevated by the Creator above the whole creation (cf. Gen 1:28; Ps 8:4–9). This requires that in social relations we guarantee the recognition of human rights and duties, and the creation of such living conditions that conform to our innate human dignity. A God-fearing society will give all people an opportunity to have a home, food, and clothing, the freedom to choose their way of life, the person they will marry, and how they will bring up their children in accordance with their beliefs. They will be free to choose their professions and to receive and exchange information. They will act in their private and public life in compliance with the standards of morality implanted by God in human nature, and thus will feel protected from any attempts on their life and encroachments on their dignity, all the while enjoying and making responsible use of this freedom.

Of special note is the importance of freedom of conscience, which implies in particular the opportunity to choose between religion and atheism. This value goes hand in hand with the importance of religious freedom, which grants people the right to profess their faith without fear or censure.

—*"The Church in Relation to Society in the Situation of Perestroika,"*
  Journal of the Moscow Patriarchate (June, 1990)

"Let us commend ourselves . . . and all our life unto Christ our God"

49 Personal ethics lie at the core of Christian morality. Addressed to all people and aimed at transfiguring human souls, the Christian message focuses on the person and his or her spiritual experience. These salutary changes of our inner life occur not in isolation from our environment, and not in some special laboratory setting. Instead, the fruit of our spiritual lives is worked out in real contact with other people: first and foremost, in our family, then at work, in society, and finally, in the state.

One cannot remain a Christian only within the four walls of one's house, in the bosom of the family, or in the solitude of a cell, and then cease being a Christian while mounting a professorial rostrum, sitting down in front of a TV camera, voting in parliament, or even proceeding with a scientific experiment. Christian motivation must stand behind everything that is within the sphere of a believer's vital interests. The faithful cannot mechanically detach their professional or scientific interests from the spiritual and moral context of their lives. ... Our religious motivation must be universal and comprehensive. Thus, a religious way of life is a mode of existence of those people whose choice is motivated and determined by the principles of their faith.

—*"The Norm of Faith as the Norm of Life," a paper read at the conference: "Orthodox Theology on the Threshold of the Third Millennium"* (February 7, 2000)

The Purpose of our Freedom

50 When St Paul calls us to liberty, he speaks of people's predestination to be free in Christ, that is, free from the manacles of sin, for man can gain true freedom only by freeing himself from sin and from the dark power of instinct and evil weighing upon him. Freedom has been granted unto men so that they can consciously choose to obey the absolute and salutary will of God. It is the path, opened up to people, of freely chosen union with God through complete obedience to him and becoming like him in holiness.

This is the meaning of the great gift of freedom. It was totally consistent with his nature that our Maker would implant in his creation both grace and a likeness to him, for which we hopefully strive, as well as the happiness of always feeling his presence "everywhere present and filling all things."[3] Of course, the

[3]From the prayer "O heavenly King."—*Ed.*

Creator could have programmed us for his all-abundant grace as easily as we set our alarm clocks. However, being the very ground and source of goodness and freedom, he kindly bestowed this property of freedom upon mankind. It is only this kind of freedom that is truly God-given.

—*"The Norm of Faith as the Norm of Life"* (February 7, 2000)

Theology: Rooted in Experience, Interpreted for Each Generation

51 In our Orthodox Christian Faith, our theology is one of ascetics and zealots of prayer—theology as spiritual contemplation of divine things. Without this lofty contemplation, rooted in actual spiritual experience, there can be no theology whatsoever in the Church. And there is also the science and discipline of theology, accumulating all the richness of church tradition, which really is and has to be the work of specialists and ecclesiastical scholars. Without developing this kind of theological knowledge and doing serious research work in cooperation with secular science, the Church cannot lead a full life either. Can one imagine the early Church without the works of the holy fathers, great Christian thinkers, and creators of Christian culture?

However, there is one more dimension of theology that I would like to dwell on.

God revealed to the Church his will for the salvation of people, and granted the means for partaking in his salvific action. However, when affected by external conditions, including views and beliefs prevailing in society, the truths of divine revelation often lose their applicability and strength. Theology is also an instrument of interpreting divine revelation, bringing to each new generation the realization that the word of God is alive and real. In this sense, theology becomes a truly creative thinking process that seeks to fulfill concrete tasks and solve real problems by relying on both the prayerful and intellectual theological wisdom that has been accumulated in the tradition of the Church.

—*Remarks at the plenary session of the Synodal Theological Commission of the Russian Orthodox Church* (May 4, 2009)

"One cannot be a Christian and not think about our world"

52 In assuming an attitude toward the world, there is no other way for the Church but to move toward it, being fully aware of the fact that the world is full of evil and pain, falsehood and injustice. Despite this, within the world are many who are at the same time striving to heal these sores and transform people, society, and the world. One cannot be a Christian and not think about our world, as it is the creation of God. It is true that sin and suffering came into our world through freedom and man's existential choice to move away from God. Nevertheless, as we continue to do Christ's work on earth, we as the Church cannot turn a blind eye to the suffering and needs of those around us.

—*"The Church and Society in the Light of the Russian Orthodox Church's Basic Social Concept," a speech in the State Duma* (2001)

How the Church Views the State

53 From the Church's point of view, the religious importance of state power lies in its ability to limit the power of evil in the world and to contribute to the affirmation of what is good (cf. Rom 13.1–7). While accomplishing its mission, the state, acting in accordance with its nature, may resort to force (cf. Rom 13.4). No other institution of human society has that right. The state can be considered sinful and criminal if it resorts to force in order to fight against good, or if it does not use this force to put an end to evil. The state's ability to suppress evil and further the good is the major criterion the Church uses for appraising the state's actions from a moral perspective.

—*"The Church and Society," a speech before the Duma* (2001)

The State is not a Law unto Itself

54 Christians must eschew absolute power, since we know that power has only earthly, temporary, and transient value, and is only necessitated by the presence of sin in the world and the need to restrain it. According to the teaching of the Church, the state also has no right to become a law unto itself, or to extend its boundaries in order to have complete autonomy from God and the order of things established by him. Indeed, when power becomes absolute, it can and does lead to the abuse of power and even to the idolization of those rulers wielding the power. Hence, a tyrant or a dictator cannot be seen as a real Christian, even if they regard themselves as such.

—*"The Church and Society," a speech before the Duma* (2001)

The Differing Goals of Church and State

55 Both the Church and the state are called to resist evil in this world and facilitate the triumph of the good. . . . Although they pursue rather similar goals in ordering people's earthly lives, there is still a very significant difference between these two institutions. The state is called to stave off human society's disintegration into a hell of lawlessness and all-permissiveness, while the Church's duty is to transform the earthly community into the kingdom of God. The Church is able to lead sinners to holiness. That is why she can—and must—further the spiritual transfiguration of the individual and society as a whole. This is beyond the state's task and would be impossible for it. The state's duty is to ensure obedience to basic rules in order to keep social relations from degrading.

—*"The Church and Society," a speech before the Duma* (2001)

Christian Economic Motives

56 Since it is an important factor in human life, economics should be both efficient and fair. It is not only the thirst for creativity, but also the desire to provide for themselves and their families, that motivates people to work. However, there should be another motive, namely, to help those who cannot support themselves. Every man should produce more than he needs, to share a surplus with the indigent (cf. Eph 4.28).

—*"The Church and Society," a speech before the Duma* (2001)

Property and Stewardship

57 The issue of property ownership presents serious economic problems; yet for the Church the nature of property is a question of minor importance. From the theological perspective, all things belong to God and are within his power as the Creator and Giver of all blessings. Christians believe that an individual, an industrial corporation, and a state all have in their earthly possession only those material goods that the Lord gives them.

Hence, in the Church's opinion, the issue of how this property is used comes to the fore. If the possession of material goods is seen only as a way to satisfy egoistic desires for personal comfort and has nothing to do with a Christian idea of helping one's neighbor, then such a use of wealth and property is certainly sinful. If a property owner causes environmental pollution or social and inter-ethnic conflict, thus ruining people's lives, then the Church cannot help but express her serious concern.

—*"The Church and Society," a speech before the Duma* (2001)

Gender Equality and Gender Roles

58 The Orthodox Church stands for gender equality, yet with the awareness that men and women are very different in their psychological and physiological nature. To disregard these obvious differences and artificially equalize the masculine and feminine natures, thus stirring up the spirit of reckless competitiveness between the two sexes, is considered a sinful act in the eyes of the Church. Women are by no means obliged to enter a boxing ring, join a football team, or even mount a weightlifting platform simply because men do it. Women have another nature given by God, and another mission. At the same time, the Church calls upon the state and society to see to it that women do not suffer gender-based discrimination.

—*"The Church and Society," a speech before the Duma* (2001)

The Church's Focus:
The Individual, not "Systems" or "Structures"

59 A crisis of the human heart and personality always lies beneath every system's crisis, and a reform of every system, every structure, and every society must begin with changing people's hearts. It is pointless to engage in the classic dispute about what is primary: the system or the individual? If we apply the gospel standard to everything, we see that Jesus Christ, as revealed to us in the gospel, was not a social reformer, but a great reformer of the human spirit. That is why he addressed neither "systems" nor "structures" in his sermons, but always the individual.

Jesus never called upon his compatriots to overthrow Roman rule, abolish slavery, or redistribute material goods, but spoke of the spiritual transfiguration of the individual and humanity as a whole. "And you shall know the truth, and the truth shall make you free," he said (Jn 8.32). "For you, brethren, have been called to liberty," St Paul echoed (Gal 5.13). What is meant here is not freedom in the social sense, nor the "liberty" and "brotherhood" that became the slogan of the French Revolution. Instead, this refers to the liberation of people from the slavery of sin and the act of uniting them into one brotherhood of many millions. Indeed, in the Church "there is neither Greek nor Jew . . . bond nor free: but Christ is all, and in all" (Col 3.11).

I am not in any way suggesting that Christians should put up with social injustice or be indifferent to the violation of civil rights and freedoms. Yet I want to emphasize that the Church should regard the spiritual and moral transformation of man as its primary task, if we want to remain faithful to the spirit of Christ's gospel.

—*"Evangelism and Culture," an address to the World Missionary Conference* (1996)

Christianity and Culture

60 The goal of Christian mission with regard to culture is not the enculturation of Christianity. Instead, we want to see a Christianization of culture that is not merely a "tactic," but which comes about because we become bearers of Christ's glad tidings. . . . We speak of culture as a means for the spiritual and moral development of humanity. If certain forms of culture and art do not contribute to our spiritual growth but instead stir up passions and instincts, leading to the disintegration of personality, then this is really a pseudo-culture, an anti-culture that cannot be an ally of the Church.

True culture should not unleash the Dionysian elements in men, whereof the ancient philosophers spoke, but should exalt people, inspire them, and bring them closer to God. What is born in a rage of passions and because of man's rebellion against the world, harmony, life, and God is not only anti-culture but anti-Christianity.... Any such anti-culture, no matter where and when it comes into being, is anti-Christian.

Saying this, I would like to emphasize that I am neither merely nostalgic for the culture of the past, nor an opponent of the new forms and phenomena of modern culture taken as they are. It is not the form but the content that is important, though the former cannot but reflect the latter to some extent. I am convinced that the Church should not blindly chase after and adapt to every new cultural trend. Nor should she reject them sweepingly, ceding to paganism complete control over all modern cultural expression.

—*"Evangelism and Culture"* (1996)

"We strive to transfigure the life of the world"

61 The whole Christian brotherhood needs to come to a broader and more daring understanding of its mission. We must discern our apostolic origins as we strive to transfigure the life of the world around us without compromise. One of my brothers in the faith, a Russian bishop, was summoned in the mid-1980s to appear before a local official in charge of promoting atheistic ideology. "Why are you inviting children to a Christmas feast?" asked the official. "It is not your job; you are to satisfy religious needs." Apparently, this man assumed that all the bishop should do is perform occasional services for old-age pensioners. The bishop said in response, "My religious need is to change the world!"

We need to come to the same understanding of our missionary service, even though as men we believe we have no chance to succeed, just as the apostles of Christ had no chance to succeed in human terms. Their mission was a success and transformed the world, inasmuch as they presented a united front that in turn united the people around them. A miracle happened! When people acted in accord, Christ acted together with them.

—*"Evangelism and Culture"* (1996)

Joys and Sorrows

62 Analyzing my life's journey, I have to say that joys and sorrows alike have been utterly necessary for personality formation and for the fullness of life. A man can establish himself as a person thanks not only to the joyful moments of life, but also to the times when it is necessary for him to overcome difficulties and bear blows. This is indeed a human life. As Christians, we are called to resist evil and affirm the good (cf. Rom 12.9)—this is what God has destined us for.

—*"Resisting Evil and Affirming the Good," an interview with* Church and Time (2001, Issue 1)

". . . rejoicing that they were counted worthy to suffer shame for his name" (Acts 5.41)

63 When I was appointed ruling bishop of the Smolensk diocese, an actor of a local drama theatre visited me and said that his father had been in prison alongside my father. At first, I refused to believe him. Yet he showed me his father's letters describing his journey from Leningrad to Kolyma, and so I realized it was true.

In the letter, his father wrote that they were being driven to prison in carriages chock-full of people. They all were dispirited, except a strange young man among them whom they called Mishenka Gundyaev. He was so joyful and cheerful, and his face was shining! When asked, "What are you rejoicing at?" he would answer, "Why should I grieve? It was not for a crime, but for being faithful to God that I have been put in prison." He carried that joy with him for the rest of his life.

—*"Resisting Evil and Affirming the Good"* (2001)

"Salvation is the goal of every Christian's life"

64 Salvation is the goal of every Christian's life. Therefore, everything Christians do, whether they work alone or in cooperation with other people, makes sense only when it serves the purpose of salvation. For Christians, the soteriological dimension is the only true dimension of human life. Similarly, a soteriological criterion is the only criterion for appraising their own and other people's deeds and those events in private and social life that affect, directly or indirectly, their spiritual life.

—*"Witness and Service," the keynote paper presented at the 10th General Assembly of SYNDESMOS* (August 1980)

How to Submit to God's Will

65 Submission to the will of God has one condition, without which it can never become a reality. This condition is man's love for his Creator. This great love exceeds everything and is exceptional, in the sense that it is above all other objects and requires exertion of all spiritual powers. Such love alone is the motivation for the submission of the human will to the will of the invisible Creator, for it gives rise to people's aspiration for full unity with God. That is why it is not just said, "Love God," but "Love . . . with all your heart, with all your soul, and with all your mind" (Mt 22.37), that is, with all your being, unreservedly and without compromise.

—*"Witness and Service"* (August 1980)

Love and Dialogue

66 I think that the very idea of dialogue is inherent in the nature of Christianity. We have no right not to talk to others, especially to those who consider themselves Christians. The central idea of Christianity is the idea of love—active love. Our Christian vocation compels us to love our neighbors. How then can we not show love for those who call themselves Christians, even if they differ from us in their theological views?

—*"Resisting Evil and Affirming the Good"* (2001)

Unity and our Witness to the World

67 I believe that striving after unity is inherent in the very nature of the Church. In his letter to Polycarp of Smyrna, Ignatius the God-Bearer wrote, "Be mindful of unity; nothing is better than this."[4] Thus, care for the unity of the Church is a primary task of episcopal ministry.

However, we should not forget that these words are addressed to all of us as well. When we face divisions, we must try to overcome them. . . . For many non-Christians, they believe that the divisions within Christianity are a sign of weakness in the Christian Church and that it is unable to unite people. Therefore, overcoming our divisions is our duty not only to ourselves, but also to the secular world and to representatives of other religions.

—*"Resisting Evil and Affirming the Good"* (2001)

Christianity Embraces Both Man and Society

68 In such an all-embracing religion as Christianity, personal and social elements find their ultimate combination, since Christian

[4]Ignatius of Antioch (†c. 107), *Letter to Polycarp* 1.2.—*Ed.*

moral teaching implies both personal improvement and the improvement of human society. However, this will by no means run counter to the assertion that Christianity is an "individual" religion in the loftiest sense of this word, for it proclaims the everlasting value of the individual adopted by God: the individual who is wise, free, and called to infinite perfection in order to acquire the kingdom of God. Hence, it is clear why Christianity attaches such importance to the moral assessment of human actions and personal virtues.

—*"Witness and Service"* (August 1980)

Freedom and Regaining the Image of God

69 Freedom reveals the divine nature in man only if and when this divine nature permeates his will. If a man wisely and freely submits his will to the will of God, he completes his destiny, revealing God's image and likeness to the extent predestined for him by the Creator. For this reason one can state that the Christian understanding of human nature and of our mission includes the idea that man gains solidarity with God through the voluntary submission of his will to the will of God. This submission makes a dignified relationship between the Creator and man created in his image possible.

—*"Witness and Service"* (August 1980)

"This seeming contradiction"

70 Christianity shifts people's interests from this visible world, or "earthly city," to the spiritual world, our "heavenly city," whose treasures alone are able to grant complete satisfaction (cf. Mt 6.19–21). Hence, one can find a paradox in the Christian attitude to the world: on the one hand, the faith calls us to forsake the world and disdain love for it; on the other hand, it calls us to love the world as God's creation and take part in perfecting it.

It is important for Christians to be aware of this seeming contradiction, and yet a rational understanding will not suffice. It is necessary to dive into the depths of the Christian faith in order to perceive empirically the reality that opens up there. As we experience life in Christ, we will realize that faith in the "heavenly city" or the "kingdom of heaven" is intertwined with faith in the exceptional value of man, destined to own this kingdom. That is why Christians here on earth, who are performing the arduous feat of preparing themselves for the heavenly kingdom, must manifest their faith and loyalty to the "heavenly city" by serving those who are to destined to inherit this city, our brothers and sisters.

—*"Witness and Service"* (August 1980)

"Everything may be done for the glory of God"

71 Living in society and as citizens of their nation, members of the Church are all called to bear witness to Christ. Creating in themselves a new man in the likeness of God through righteousness and the sanctity of truth, they must show the beauty of this new creation in their social and cultural milieu. Christians are required to play an active part in the life of society, loving their fellow citizens and their earthly homeland with sincerity, so that faith in Christ and the life of the Church may not be alien to their nation.

Any attempt to set up a false dichotomy between religious life and active participation in the life of society is erroneous. This falsehood was condemned by the Old Testament prophets (cf. Is 58.1–12) and even more expressly by our Lord and Savior himself (cf. Mt 23.3–23). Christians are called to combine their secular and religious activities, so that everything may be done for the glory of God.

—*"Witness and Service"* (August, 1980)

The Church Speaks to All

72 While performing her prophetic ministry, the Church comes in contact with other religions and ideologies. Being faithful to the call of her divine Head even "unto the end of the world" (Mt 28.18–20), she has always since apostolic times been bearing her witness with wisdom and good sense. It is pertinent to recall St Paul's preaching before the Areopagus (Acts 17.22–31). Bearing this witness implies, among other things, respect for the spiritual and moral principles by which even non-Christians are guided in their search for the good and for justice. Addressing the world with her prophetic words full of humility, wisdom, and love, and supporting these words with her vigorous and active profession of faith, the Church is called to multiply good everywhere, spreading it to all spheres of human life, so that nothing is left to the tyranny of evil forces.

—*"Witness and Service"* (August 1980)

"The Church can heal . . . ethnic intolerance"

73 By virtue of the grace given to it by its Founder and Head Jesus Christ, the Church can heal vices and imperfections tormenting society, including the social imperfection of ethnic intolerance. The Church first of all brings peace to human souls and thus helps spread peace and love between neighbors. Actually, a peaceful attitude toward other ethnic groups starts within hearts that have love for their neighbors, while a lack of peace and love results in anger and acts of ethnic intolerance.

—*"Seek the Spirit of Peace and thousands will be saved around you,"*
an address to the 9th World Russian People's Council
(March 2005)

Love and the Mystery of the Cross

74 We cannot grasp the depth and the power of both divine thoughts and divine works. We can only make our hearts receptive to these thoughts and works. Once we do so, we begin to understand what Christ means for each of us; this understanding is gained not by well-turned formulas—for no formula is sufficient to express God's design—but by our hearts.

By accepting God's word, man assumes the power of faith, so those who have found Christ begin to understand that it is only love that can explain the mystery of the cross and the suffering of the almighty God. This mystery can be explained neither in terms of obligation on the part of God, for God owes no one anything, nor in terms of magical power, for God saves no one automatically, but only in terms of love.

—*Homily on the feast of the Exaltation of the Holy Cross*
(September 27, 2010)

"How can we stop telling lies?"

75 The Christian way of life must rigorously exclude any lies. If we tell lies, then we carry out the work of the devil. On the contrary, it is veracity, honesty, and sincerity that provide the most convincing and absolute proof of one's firm faith. However, if certain conditions, our weakness, the wrong upbringing, or the influence of those around us still cause us to commit the sin of

lying, how can we correct this vice? How can we stop telling lies?

St John Climacus, whose work we frequently cite during the first week of Great Lent, since he possessed such deep insight into the mysteries of human growth, writes: "He who has obtained the fear of the Lord has forsaken lying, having within himself an incorruptible judge—his own conscience."[5]

—*Homily on Wednesday of the First Week of Lent* (February 17, 2010)

"A real worldview challenge"

76 One task of the Church today is to encourage people . . . to accept faith not as a historical tradition, or as part of some nice and pleasant folk culture that immerses them in a cozy romantic atmosphere of the past, but as a real worldview challenge. People today should realize that the existence of their civilization largely depends on how eagerly they will embrace God's truth in their hearts and minds.

—*Interview on "National Interest," a show on the TV channel*
   Russia-1 (November 21, 2009)

Where Human Divisions are Overcome and Salvation is Found

77 The Church is not only a place for our meeting with God but for a special meeting of people. Through partaking of the one bread and one cup we become a single whole, and this mystical unity of people overcomes all of our differences, whether social, material, ethnic, or political. While the world gives us example upon example of divisions, which have multiplied over the course

---

[5]John Climacus, *Ladder* 12.7. *The Ladder of Divine Ascent*, Lazarus Moore, trans. (Boston, MA: Holy Transfiguration Monastery, 2001), 94.

of history, the Church offers a place for people to unite and to stand together before God. The Church is the place where human divisions are mystically and truly overcome.

That is why we say that there is no salvation outside the Church. It is true for every person, but also true for the whole of human history. Whatever place the Church may statistically occupy in the human race today, it is only in this flock, great or small, that the mystery of salvation, and the great mystery of the human race standing together before God, are accomplished.

—*Homily on Saturday of the First Week of Lent* (February 20, 2010)

The Vocation of Women in the Church

78 It is my deep conviction that today, Orthodox women should assume a proactive public attitude as guardians of Christian moral values in the family and society. Along with their calling as wives and mothers, Christian women should be full-fledged members of civil society, since they are responsible for the destiny of the country. They must be actively involved in all areas of social life so that the voice of the faithful may be heard.

At the same time, the role of wife, mother, and keeper of the hearth should not be deformed in any circumstances, because it is the real physical and spiritual foundation of the human community. Nothing can be sacrificed in our commitment to the values of family and motherhood, since these are the values on which the existence of human civilization depends.

—*Address at the opening of the First Forum of Orthodox Women* (December 3, 2009)

True Human Freedom

79 The Lord says, "And you shall know the truth, and the truth shall make you free," and to the Jews who insisted that they had never been slaves he says, "Most assuredly, I say to you, whoever commits sin is a slave of sin" (Jn 8.34). These words reveal the profound meaning of human life and history. No external freedoms can liberate man; no external declarations can make man free. It is easy to enslave him and his mind, to inculcate stereotypes and prejudice into him, and to set his thinking and his will to a required direction, if his will becomes a slave of sin and passions. And if we learn how to rule over our passions and sin, we can rule over the whole world. . . .

It should not be supposed that this is something new or something characteristic of our time only. If it had been so, Christ would have never said these mind-burning words about true human freedom. It is exactly to correct this false understanding of slavery and freedom from sin that our Lord came down to earth, then to Golgotha, and ultimately came to redeem the human race. Christ brings God's truth to the world, the truth that makes us free.

—*Homily on the feast of the Synaxis of the New Martyrs of Butovo*
(May 1, 2010)

"God does not distinguish between big and small problems"

80 Everyone should remember that there are no big or small problems before God. With God, there are no strong, masterful, outstanding, rich or—on the contrary—untalented, poor, or sick people. God has his children, and each one turns to God with a problem that is painful. For one it is a matter of weighty and consequential public policy, while for another the problem is a matter of relations with a neighbor, a family member, or a co-worker. Man is constituted so that the greatest problems facing heads of state and governments and our ordinary human problems equally pain the heart.

That is why God does not distinguish between big and small problems, between the great man and the smallest one. Our whole inner life, our joy and our pain alike, are open before God, and he responds to the joy and the pain of anyone. That is why you should turn to God with continued prayer for everything: when you are late for a train, suffer a setback in life, fall ill, face family grief, or fail at work.

—*Homily on the Fourth Sunday after Pascha* (April 25, 2010)

How to Conquer Envy

81 How do we overcome envy? St Tikhon of Zadonsk said, "Pride is the mother of envy. Mortify a mother, and her daughter will perish." To overcome the feeling of envy one has to overcome one's pride. But since pride fully reveals the very nature of sin, it is very difficult to struggle with this vice, and it is only by the power of God that a person can overcome pride. Therefore, prayer and participation in the sacraments of the Church, continued reflection on one's own life and the movements of one's soul and one's thoughts, and the strict judgment of oneself can help you to overcome pride.

However, there are two more remarkable remedies.

The first is the awareness of the fact that the Lord has endowed each individual with unique qualities, and there are no two absolutely similar persons. Each individual is unique and has his or her own value before God. However weak, sick, or unlucky one can seem, he has infinite value in God's eyes. The awareness of this fact helps a person to refrain from envy. The world is vast, and everyone in this world has his or her own place. The awareness of the unique nature of each person and the divine design for man helps to overcome the feeling of envy.

There is another very important remedy, which is the practice of doing good works. When we do something good for a person, he or she ceases to be distant from us, and becomes close. We do not envy those to whom we have done something good. If some doubt it, let them do something good to a person whom they envy, and the envy will gradually pass away, because this person will become dear to them.

—*Homily on Monday of the First Week of Lent* (February 15, 2010)

What Will We Regret on Our Deathbed?

82 On our deathbed, none of us will grieve over the lost opportunity to earn another thousand euros or dollars. I have had to hear the confessions of dying people, but I have never heard them grieve over anything material that they failed to gain in life. Exactly at this moment, a single, absolutely correct system of values is formed, because all the worldly things recede to the background, and the only thing that a person can mourn is that he failed to do good deeds, that he offended someone, or that he neglected to do his duty.

—*Address to the 14th World Russian People's Council* (May 25, 2010)

Only One Criterion

83 It seems to me that there must be only one criterion, the most important and fundamental one, for assessing what is happening to us and to understand what will happen to us. It is the state of our human personality! All the rest is secondary. But why is this? Because God, in creating man, put his image into him. We are bearers of divine qualities. God is absolute reason, and he has bequeathed man a part of this reason. God is absolute freedom, and man has received the gift of freedom. Man breaks away from the course of necessity in which the whole universe is immersed, and is the only creature that possesses the divine gift of freedom.

For this reason it seems to me that it is man who must be the criterion for understanding life. Yet what exactly about man is the criterion? Can it be his passions or vices, or the transient fashions of the day? Of course not! The criterion can be found only in the divine nature that is present in man—the image of God in him. Freedom is one of the manifestations of this image of God. Because of this, the notions of human freedom and dignity can be used as a universal measuring stick to aid us in assessing what is happening to people in the human community today.

—*Address at Yerevan State University* (March 18, 2010)

"To see the divine power . . . try to live by this word"

84 In order to see the divine power in the word of the Savior, it is necessary to try to live by this word (cf. Jn 7.17). Then we begin to acquire an inner spiritual experience of such poignant power that it overcomes any human power. Sometimes it seems to people that it is so difficult to follow Christ, so difficult to hear and fulfill his word. Yet it is only an apparent difficulty. In reality, "my yoke is easy and my burden is light" (Mt 11.30). And if we take in the good news brought by the Savior, if we take the gospel's words to heart, then we acquire an easy and saving burden, and begin to live by the divine design as God has willed us to live. Then in the joys of this life, in this heaven-like existence, our sorrows, our weaknesses, and our sins disappear, and in our heavenly inner world, we experience real communion with God.

—*Homily on the Sunday after Nativity* (January 10, 2010)

Being "Rich toward God"

85 What does being "rich toward God" (Lk 12.21) mean? First of all, it implies that we have the right guideline for life, and have put our lives into God's right hand. We see God as the center of life and we seek to live according to the truth and the law of God. Then material wealth does not only improve one's living conditions, but also helps one to build spiritual wealth, which does not cease when the human heart stops beating and goes to eternity. When our wealth or even modest income enables us to be strong and sensible enough to give to the needy, to share with the poor, and to do good works, then these material temporal values gain eternal importance, because they serve the eternal values of the heavenly kingdom. This is what being "rich toward God" means.

—*Homily on the feast of the Holy Prince Alexander Nevsky*
(December 6, 2009)

"Bear one another's burdens" (Gal 6.2)

86 There can be no love without sacrifice, no love without joyful service to others. It is not accidental that in the reading from Galatians we find the remarkable words: "Bear one another's burdens, and so fulfill the law of Christ" (Gal 6.2). Where then do we learn to bear one another's burdens? . . . Where can one open one's soul to reveal the most beautiful qualities of one's soul? Where can one take upon oneself the burdens of another and thus fulfill the law of Christ? Only there, where love is—in the family.

—*Homily on the feast of the Holy Prince Peter and Princess Fevronia*
(July 8, 2010)

"Never beat your head against a brick wall"

87 Living side by side with such a human giant as Metropolitan Nikodim (Rotov) was, I realized afterwards, perhaps the most important foundation of my life. From him, I learned how the Church should act to make her mission a success. He taught me this: even ravens do not fly straight. They seek to bypass airflows. Therefore, never beat your head against a brick wall, but look for a way to bypass the wall without changing your intention. I observed many times how my teacher would bypass impregnable walls, while remaining absolutely faithful to the Russian Orthodox Church in everything.

—*"Metropolitan Kirill: I have Committed Myself to the Hands of God," interview on Radonezh.ru* (June 30, 2005)

Cured by St John of Kronstadt's Prayers

88 My mother often used to take me to the closed St John's Monastery along the Karpovka River. At the bricked-up window right over the place where Fr John of Kronstadt was buried, there was a policeman posted to keep the faithful away. My mother and I waited till the policeman moved away for a short time, then ran up to the window, knelt, and prayed.

Once I fell seriously ill with severe pneumonia. The illness did not yield even to penicillin. My parents were gravely concerned. When I felt very sick, I asked to take the picture of Fr John of Kronstadt from the wall. At that time he was not canonized yet and wore a red velvet robe with blue lapels. I kissed the cold glass, held the photograph to my forehead, and prayed and prayed and prayed. The next day I fully recovered. I have no doubt that it was through the intercessions of Fr John.

—*"I have Committed Myself to the Hands of God"* (June 30, 2005)

"This great ideal"

89 Metropolitan Nikodim (Rotov) was a man of the Church. It means that he was a man of the world in the original catholic sense. Like Martin Luther King Jr., he could say, "I have a dream." His dream was the powerful unity of all the followers of Christ and the reunification of the Christian *oikoumene* in the modern world on the basis of the Scriptures and the tradition of the early and undivided Church of the apostolic age. It is not his fault that this great ideal has remained unattainable in the human community, since we are dulled by sin and divided. "No great effort is needed to usher in division. What is needed for unity are truly heroic efforts and, along with that, special help from God," His Eminence used to say.

—*Speech at the conference dedicated to the 30th anniversary of the repose of Met. Nikodim (Rotov)* (September 4, 2008)

Two Secret Liturgies

90 My late teacher Metropolitan Nikodim (Rotov) celebrated two secret liturgies, which I happened to witness.

The metropolitan celebrated one of these liturgies at a wall that was dented with bullets, at the place where prisoners of the Solovki Camp (now known as the Russian Golgotha) were executed by shooting. Another liturgy was at the former monastic Valaam Island, amidst the looted and defaced cemetery church defiled by blasphemers. The metropolitan believed it absolutely necessary for him to celebrate there despite everything. He saw in it a spiritual need and considered it his lofty duty.

I will remind you that it was the most smoldering and hopeless time of stagnation, when the so-called ordinary Soviet people had been steeped in atheistic education since their childhood. If they caught clergy "red-handed" they would at best, without further ado, take us to a police station, and at worst would mock the celebrant and the sacrament. However, by God's mercy neither of these things happened. And these two secret liturgies, in which I had the good fortune to assist, continue to live in my memory as the most powerful religious experiences of my life.

—*30th anniversary of the repose of Met. Nikodim* (September 4, 2008)

The Life of a Patriarch

91 In a patriarch's life there can be nothing personal, nothing private. He himself and all his life belong to God and the Church. His heart bleeds for the people of God, especially those who have fallen away from the Church and those who have not yet found faith. The patriarchal service is a special spiritual feat. It is impossible to accomplish this feat single-handedly or only with the support of a limited circle of like-minded people. Involved in this feat through communion in prayer and collegial work are the entire episcopate and the fullness of the Church in all the variety of gifts peculiar to her members.

—*Speech at the Patriarchal Enthronement* (February 1, 2009)

The Beauty and Truth of Orthodoxy Must Touch People's Everyday Lives

92 The beauty of Orthodoxy and her witness to the truth can be accepted and assimilated only if people become clearly aware of the importance of this witness for their personal, family, and social life, and learn to couple the eternal words of God with the realities of everyday life with its concerns, joys, and sorrows.

To couple the Orthodox faith and the gospel's morals with everyday thoughts, aspirations, and people's hopes is to help them answer today's most complicated philosophical and ethical questions. The faith will become comprehensible, despite all the diverse and contradictory views and convictions existing in society, only when a person becomes aware and begins to deeply feel the unquestionable rightness and power of the message God himself sends to us through his revelation. Human thought and the human word cannot be more powerful than the word of God. And if this obvious truth does not become evident to many people, it is only because the beauty and cogency of God's word is darkened by what we call "the human factor" today.

—*Speech at the Patriarchal Enthronement* (February 1, 2009)

"Not only sermons"

93 The Church's witness before the world presupposes not only sermons from the pulpit, but also an open and motivated dialogue in which both sides speak and listen. Through this dialogue the truths of the faith become understandable, for they come into creative and living contact with people's ideas and beliefs. At the same time, through this dialogue the Church enriches herself with knowledge of what modern man is, and what he thinks and asks of the Church.

This dialogue helps people of different views and beliefs, including religious ones, to understand one another, and promotes civic peace and harmony.

—*Speech at the Patriarchal Enthronement* (February 1, 2009)

"Faith is different from knowledge"

94 Faith is different from knowledge. A person's knowledge is based on his experience and sensations. Therefore, a visible object becomes an object of knowledge, not of faith. A word heard is not an object of faith either, but becomes an object of knowledge.

However, faith is confidence that there is something that cannot be physically sensed. . . . One can come to the idea of God logically, discovering the Creator for oneself, but this discovery is not yet faith. The idea of God that develops in one's conscience must lead to a change in one's spirit, taking root in one's soul; not only in one's mind, but also in the heart. Thus, faith is a special state of the soul. It belongs to the inner spiritual life of a human being, dwelling within the human heart.

—*A Pastor's Word* (Moscow: DECR, 2008), 6–7

We cannot answer "Why?"

95 The Creator's design for the world and for man is an inscrutable mystery for us. We cannot fathom it or rationally understand it. We will never be able to answer the question: Why has God willed to order the life of this world and to determine the course of human history in this, and not any other, way?

In this respect, all kinds of daring questions arise: Why? What for? What is the goal? However, precisely these questions often prevent us from finding faith. "Why does God allow evil? Why did he want by all means to suffer for the sake of our salvation?" Unable to understand this mystery, we can only reverently bow before its inscrutability and say in our hearts: "I believe, O Lord, for it has been accomplished according to your word."

—*A Pastor's Word* (Moscow: DECR, 2008), 83

"My grandfather was a real confessor of the faith"

96 When I was young, I had no need to search after some special path to God and the Church, since the Lord blessed me to be born and raised in a family with strong Orthodox traditions. Both my father and grandfather were priests, though my father was ordained earlier than my grandfather. My grandfather was a real confessor of the faith and spent many years in prisons, labor camps, and exile. Once he made calculations and it turned out that he had been in forty-seven prisons and had been exiled seven times.

My grandfather was a technician and locomotive driver at the Moscow-Kazan railway. He was paid a good wage and he donated much to Christian shrines on Mt Athos and in Jerusalem. Several years ago I was on Mt Athos and found the names of all my relatives in one of the monasteries' prayer list; the monks commemorate us as benefactors to this day.

My grandfather was a very courageous and strong man. He raised one orphan and seven children of his own. And in spite of all this, he voluntarily underwent severe trials and deprivations by speaking out against the closure of churches during the atheistic persecution.

—*"I have Taken my Appointment to Smolensk as an Important Service Entrusted to me by God," an interview in* Smolensk (2006, Issue 11)

Marriage and Monasticism

97 I have never regretted my choice of monasticism because such was the will of God for my path. Finishing seminary and thinking over whether to be a married priest or a monk, I decided that if the Lord blessed me with a girl who would become the happiness of all my life, then I would lead her to the altar. If such a meeting didn't happen, it meant the Lord wished me to become a monk. This was how my life path was determined at the age of twenty-two.

"He who is unmarried cares for the things of the Lord—how he may please the Lord. But he who is married cares about the things of the world—how he may please his wife," St Paul says

(1 Cor 7.32–33). This verse contains, in my view, the apostle's idea of the advantage of the monastic path. The Church understands monasticism as a spiritual feat, requiring endless spiritual effort. However, all people cannot and must not become monks, just as not all of them are obliged to marry. At the moment of the great choice of one's path, one should listen to what the Lord calls him to. The heavenly Father has many dwellings (cf. Jn 14.2), and a married believer will always find a mode of life that will enable him to honestly serve God, his family, and his neighbors, and to live by God's commandments. The married status and the monastic path of the Orthodox Christian are equal in the eyes of the Church, provided his faith is firm and effective.

—*"Metropolitan Kirill: Russia is Entering a New Era," an interview in* Trud (December 27, 2006)

Dialogue without Compromise

98 Church tradition teaches us that it is possible and important to assert Orthodoxy through both the ascetical experience of the rejection of the world and the use of a mode of thinking more characteristic of secular philosophy or scientific and cultural achievements. The holy fathers sought to bring the Church to the external world by accepting all that is beneficial in this world and rejecting all things sinful. To this end they maintained continued dialogue with the state and society, even when the state and society were not Christian. That is why today, just as in the times of the holy fathers, dialogue with the external world is not a betrayal of Orthodoxy, but rather a means of bringing Christian values into the life of society.

It is very important that in our communication with people outside the Church, however, we should not be tempted to put human reason above the word of God. We should be always guided by the apostolic words: "Whether it is right in the sight of

God to listen to you more than to God, you judge" (Acts 4.19). To be guided by this important principle today, we need more courage than we did in the past, for quite often ideas directly contradicting the word of God become attractive for many due to financial, organizational, or even political support; or due to fashions or stereotypes implanted in the mass consciousness.

—*Speech at the 16th International Christmas Educational Readings* (January 29, 2008)

Neither Compromise nor Isolation

99 Witness to the Orthodox faith has always been the principal meaning of external church work. The content of this witness never changes. However, each generation of workers in the field should bear witness creatively, as new circumstances of time arise. The preservation of the true faith through history presupposes a way of handing it down to the next generation in a cultural context that will help people assimilate the salvific truths of this faith as a norm of life.

It has never been a simple task to preserve the apostolic faith. Christians have always had to avoid two extremes. On the one hand, they could not take a compromising approach to the spirit of this world in order to avoid submission to it. On the other hand, a Christian could not build a wall around himself—a fence between himself and the world that needs to hear the good news of salvation. Both self-isolation and the path of compromise are equally ruinous for Christianity.

To make witness effective, it is necessary, along with the purity of the faith, to preserve the unity of the Church. In this unity lies the power of Christianity's impact on the world. As our Savior says, "That they may be one as you, Father, are in me, and I in you; that they also may be one in us, that the world may believe that you sent me" (Jn 17.21). The preservation of church unity is a calling for all the faithful, but in the first place a calling for the episcopate.

The witness to Orthodoxy before the world presupposes the need to embrace all of human life in both its personal and social dimensions. This requires efforts to build relations not only with individuals but also with various social forces. These relations have value to the extent that they are filled with a content that can contribute to the cause of salvation. Therefore, the most important task of the Church's external work is to formulate the Orthodox attitude to the pressing problems of today.

—*"Orthodox Unity and Orthodox Witness in the World Today," an address to the Bishops' Council of the Russian Orthodox Church* (June 2008)

How to Grow Spiritually

100 There are certain conditions under which the human person can develop within himself religious feeling and acquire the power of faith. Again we turn to the analogy of having an ear for music, which every person possesses to some degree. Even he who has been told that he is tone-deaf is capable under certain conditions of developing within himself an ear for music and of learning to feel musical harmony. Imagine two people with identical musical abilities, one of whom studies music and develops these abilities, while the other works in a forge where it is not only impossible to develop an ear for music, but even difficult to preserve one's normal sense of hearing. What would be the result of this? The person who perfects his musical abilities will attain success, while the one who works in the forge would hardly become a musician.

So there are certain spiritual and moral conditions for the development of religious feeling. In the first instance they are the purity of the mind, soul, and heart of the human person. "Blessed are the pure in heart, for they shall see God" (Mt 5.8). St Isaac the Syrian writes: "Faith requires a pure and simple way of thinking."[6] Divine wisdom can never enter a bitter soul or an impure mind and a heart sullied by sin. The light can never be mixed with darkness, or purity with filth. An unsullied moral feeling and the ability to distinguish good from evil and to submit one's life to truth are the prerequisite conditions for the knowledge of God.

—*A Pastor's Word* (Moscow: DECR, 2008), 8–9

God's Law

101 The moral law as established by God regulates the human person's inner life. In following its norms, we arrange our life in accordance with God's plan, acquiring inner peace and joy. The law teaches us how to act in order to preserve the integrity of our life and bring harmony to the relationship between the spiritual and physical elements. If the human person observes this law in his personal, family, public, and professional life, and in all other activities, then he is traveling on the true path and is developing and perfecting himself.

When we transgress the law of physical being and harm our body, we experience pain. The same occurs when we transgress the moral law: pain visits us and we suffer. Put differently, when we act against the moral law, we condemn ourselves to suffering, for we destroy the inner harmony with which God has blessed human nature.

—*A Pastor's Word* (Moscow: DECR, 2008), 39

---

[6]Isaac the Syrian, *Ascetical Homilies*, Homily 52: "But faith requires a way of thinking that is single, limpidly pure and simple, far removed from any deviousness or invention of methods." *The Ascetical Homilies of Saint Isaac the Syrian* (Boston, MA: Holy Transfiguration Monastery, 2011), 391.

The Meaning of Salvation

102 The goal of our existence is to be with God, to be assimilated to God, to live in accord with the divine moral law and—thanks to this—achieve harmony in our spiritual and physical elements, equilibrium of the soul, tranquility, joy, peace, and well-being. This fullness of life is called salvation in the language of the Church. To acquire this fullness means not only to find it in this temporary life, but also, through the immortality of the soul, to bring it over to eternity.

—*A Pastor's Word* (Moscow: DECR, 2008), 41

Who is able to accept Christ?

103 Who worshiped Jesus Christ? Who accepted him? It was both the most simple and unlearned of people—the shepherds—and the most learned and wise of men—the magi. Who did not receive the newly born Christ but instead sought his destruction? A ruler and politician, ready to make human sacrifices to satisfy his lust for power—Herod.

What does this difference—between those who received Christ who came into the world, and those who rejected him—teach us? A great deal, including an awareness of the fact that Christ is revealed both in the simplicity of the human heart and in the purity of moral sensibility, and also in great human wisdom and great knowledge. As an evasive and vulgar person is not capable of receiving Christ, so too those who pursue false, illusory, and sinful ends are not capable of uniting with him either.

—*A Pastor's Word* (Moscow: DECR, 2008), 111

When Man Meets God

104 When, how, and under what circumstances can man meet with God? First and foremost, he meets God in prayer. If the prayer is sincere, wholehearted, and full of repentance; if it changes the heart; if all of a sudden tears well up in the eyes of a strong man—it means that in a moment of deep penitential prayer the soul was in such a state that God could touch it. . . .

Can such a meeting take place in prayer only? Sometimes people experience a wondrous inward change when contemplating the beauty of the world around them and feeling the harmony of life that is manifested, among other things, in human creativity. There are such remarkable works of art—in painting, sculpture and architecture—that leave no one indifferent. Enjoying their marvelous forms and perceiving their most profound harmony, one feels that he or she gets a glimpse of another world. Is this a delusion or, perhaps, a spiritual deception? Not at all, for God's very nature is harmony, and he has willed to lay the law of harmony in the foundation of the life of the universe. This law is in everything, be it elementary particles or the macrocosm. . . .

However, there is another very special realm in which we can meet with the Lord, and this is in the holy Eucharist. When we, with a contrite heart and pure thoughts and having reconciled with our neighbors, especially those with whom we were in conflict, come to the holy chalice and experience God's grace, the invisible divine power touches our hearts. It has nothing to do with any self-suggestion, physical beauty, or the skill with which the choir sings. All the external things are secondary to the wonderful melody of our heart's meeting with God.

—*Homily on Meatfare Sunday* (February 15, 2015)

"A broad coalition"

105 Today the preaching of the Orthodox Church aims at establishing interdependence and interaction between freedom and morality in accordance with the theology of the holy fathers. The right to life, fair trial, and work are truly important to social and political life because they are based on Christian ideals. Yet of no less importance is the task of maintaining moral standards, which should be taken into account when laws are enacted and policy is shaped. In relaying this message to the modern world, the Orthodox Church can rely on a broad coalition made up of traditional Christian churches, traditional religions, and conservative social currents.

—*"God's Design for Man and Freedom of Will: an Eschatological Perspective," a paper at the International Theological Conference on the Eschatological Teaching of the Church* (November 2005)

The Value of the Human Being

106 In a Christian culture, the value of the human being is objective and invariable. Man belongs to the God-created world, about which he said, "It is good" (Gen 1.25). However, the Lord singled man out from the rest of creation. In Genesis we read that he blessed the first human beings (cf. Gen 1.28), thus showing his good will to mankind. As we know, God's favor has timeless power. Thus, the value of man is determined by his value in the eyes of the Lord and confirmed by his seal—the image of God himself, inherent in human nature.

—*"Human Rights and Moral Responsibility," in* Church and Time (2006, Issue 2)

We Cannot Always Discern Good and Evil

107 Christianity disputes that people on their own are always able to make choices that serve them well, or to discern good and evil. This happens not because man himself is foolish, but because his mind, will, and feelings are affected by sin. He therefore can err in setting his life goals. The tragedy is that man might still be aware that good and evil exist, but he is not always able to tell one from the other. God helps people preserve this ability through his revelation, which contains the well-known set of moral rules recognized by almost all religious traditions.

—*"Human Rights and Moral Responsibility"* (2006)

Man is not the Measure of All Things

108 A believer would question the thesis that moral anthropocentrism is an all-pervading principle regulating the life of society and the individual. Conscience is the main criterion for discerning good from evil. It is the voice of God, helping people discern the moral law implanted by him in their nature. Yet this voice also can be drowned out by sin. That is why, in order to make a moral choice, people need to use external criteria as well—first and foremost, the God-given commandments.

—*"Human Rights and Moral Responsibility"* (2006)

The Need for Moral Foundations

109 Today, the absolute power of the state, characteristic of the modern age, is making way for the absolute power of the individual's sovereignty and human rights, regardless of any moral responsibility. This can undermine the very foundations of contemporary civilization and even destroy it. It is widely known that violation of the moral law led many powerful civilizations to collapse and, as a result, they perished from the earth. For man cannot live outside a moral context.

—*"Human Rights and Moral Responsibility"* (2006)

A Balance Between Extremes

110 Unstable and inhumane is the society in which the individual is treated with disdain while all his or her rights belong to the state and community. Yet equally inhumane is the society in which human rights become an instrument of stirring up base impulses and in which notions of good and evil are replaced by the idea of moral autonomy and pluralism. Such a society loses its moral influence on the individual. A civilized society should maintain a balance between these two extremes, being aware that every man has a timeless value inherent in his nature and, at the same time, is called to grow in dignity, bearing both legal and moral responsibility for his deeds.

—*"Human Rights and Moral Responsibility"* (2006)

"Creativity is granted to people by God"

111 Speaking about culture means, first of all, speaking about creativity and its role in people's life. Creativity, inherent in the human spirit, is characteristic of every man. Thanks to this ability, there is tremendous variety in the customs, social structures, and political systems of any given society. To Christians, it is obvious that creativity is granted to people by God. God has brought this world into being; therefore, man, created in his image and likeness, is also able to create, unlike the rest of creation. That is why it is necessary to develop creativity, so that it can play its proper part in the life of man and society.

—*"Creativity and Freedom," a speech at the conference:*
   "Christianity. Culture. Moral Values" (June 2007)

Creativity and Freedom

112 Creativity is impossible without freedom of the human spirit. A voluntary interest in various spheres of human life predisposes a person to creativity. Yet a person's creativity cannot blossom to its full extent if man acts under pressure or compulsion. Freedom inevitably raises the question of the purpose of creativity. Many prominent Russian and European thinkers have reflected on the correlation between freedom and the purpose of creativity. What benefit does it bring to the author and what impact does it have on his soul? How does a human creation affect other people? These are not idle questions, since creativity can either enrich the author's life or cause suffering and even ruin.

—*"Creativity and Freedom"* (June 2007)

"The highest freedom"

113 Man's ability to orient his will in a certain direction is an important trait and a highly ranked merit of his nature. Nevertheless, the highest freedom lies not in the ability to choose between good and evil, but in choosing good and allowing divine grace into the space of one's personal freedom; in other words, to voluntarily make room for God in one's life.

This understanding of freedom is rooted in the apostolic tradition, especially as developed by St Paul. The essence of this doctrine is captured in a well-known phrase from his letter to the Galatians: "For you, brethren, have been called to liberty; only do not use liberty as an opportunity for the flesh, but through love serve one another" (Gal 5.13).

—*"God's Design for Man and Freedom of Will"* (November 2005)

What Sort of Creativity Should We Support?

114 Only such creative activity that is able to promote unity in society, inspire people to work and lead an active life, and foster spiritual and material culture deserves public support. In other words, the purpose of creativity is to help people improve themselves, as well as their family and social relations. One ought to see his or her flaws and try to correct them. Those manifestations of creativity that run counter to these values should not be promoted in society or enjoy public and state support.

—*"Creativity and Freedom"* (June 2007)

The Foundation for Dialogue

115 The Church is a vessel containing the light. Yet this light shines far beyond her borders, enlightening "every man coming into the world" (Jn 1.9). It was this property of light, which is the grace of the Holy Spirit, that the holy apostle and evangelist John referred to when writing, "The wind blows where it wishes" (Jn 3.8). We do not mean to say that Christ's light only shines within the church walls, but it is our firm belief that the source of this light is in the Church, which is the body of Christ (cf. Col 1.24).

Thanks to this understanding of the light, we treat other religious experiences and traditions with respect, bearing in mind at the same time the words of the gospel that "he who believes and is baptized will be saved; but he who does not believe will be condemned" (Mk 16.16). It is in this spirit that we hold inter-faith dialogues. We believe they are important for gaining better understanding not only of other religious traditions, but of our own tradition as well.

—*"The Light of Christ and the Church," an address to the 3rd European Inter-Christian Assembly: "The Light of Christ Enlightens All: Hope for Renewal and Unity in Europe"* (September 5, 2007)

"In your light shall we see light" (Ps 35.10)

116 Christ's teaching is light, for it makes clear and visible what would be vague and dark without it. This light helps people come to the right understanding of God, man, and the world. No doubt we can acquire considerable knowledge by studying nature and the world on our own, but such knowledge cannot provide us with a broader perspective. If we acknowledge the existence of something that stands above human nature, then we should admit that it can only become known when it reveals itself to people. We would never be able to see what we look like, were it not for light that comes not from us, but from an independent source.

—*"The Light of Christ and the Church"* (September 5, 2007)

"Without God, it is impossible to arrive at absolute truth"

117 To me it is very clear that to live in harmony with truth in general, to live in harmony with one's own truth, or to judge other people based on one's own understanding of what truth is, are three very different matters. Not every human idea of what is right and proper is the ultimate truth. It cannot be absolute. But is it a matter of taste, then? How would you like your tea—with sugar or lemon? Each of us selects what we like the most, what we consider to be correct. If we are to follow this line of thought to its logical end, we will have to admit that we cannot hold to such notions as good and evil, but only a plurality of opinions and views. . . .

Of course, absolute truth does exist. It is the law of God. God gave us freedom and an innate sense of morality, embodied in our consciousness. Both can be used in different ways. It is important to realize that without God, it is impossible to arrive at absolute truth. Nor is there a different understanding of justice. In the modern world this word is often uttered thoughtlessly. Of course, abusing the weak is wrong. So is theft. Yet what if my truth denies yours? If I am strong, perhaps I decide that for this sole reason I can hurt anyone else and lay hands on anything that may come my way. . . .

By denying divine truth we ruin the world!

—*"By Denying Divine Truth We Ruin the World," an interview with the news agency TASS* (March 10, 2015)

Sin, Confession, and our Relationship with God

118 Repentance is a great and intricate internal effort and analysis of self, an impartial interior gaze in which one comes face to face with one's own conscience. When a person comes to confession, he or she merely completes this work and is held accountable to God.

This is very important for retaining a relationship with God. Sin is the sole obstacle that can impair this connection with him; neither rational doubts nor anything else can keep us from God, just sin alone. A sin that is not confessed is like a wall of concrete, and God's grace is unable to get through. On the other hand, in response to our repentance, God's grace heals us and we are granted the forgiveness of our sins.

—*"By Denying Divine Truth We Ruin the World"* (March 10, 2015)

Repentance

119 How can I explain the importance of repentance? The one who has lost the ability to repent is like a piano player who no longer has an ear for music. In principle, it may be possible to perform a piece of music using the notes only, but the impression will be terrible. Repentance is like a continuous self-tuning, an opportunity to take a critical look at one's actions and to avoid mistakes.

The one who ceases repenting also stops developing and perfecting one's self. Figuratively speaking, that person loses the ability to hear and begins to feel confused about sounds, noises, bombastic words, and rhetoric. In all religious traditions, repentance involves a very specific action. In Christianity it is the sacrament of confession, which helps a human being to develop the ability to repent, to keep one's finger on one's spiritual pulse, and to control one's moral condition.

—*"By Denying Divine Truth We Ruin the World"* (March 10, 2015)

"In my younger years"

120 I have doubts about many things, but I have never doubted the existence of God. I did have questions in my younger years. I used to read a lot then. My father had an excellent library. Whenever he had a spare penny, he would spend it on books. By the age of fifteen I had become familiar with works by Berdyayev, Frank, and Florensky. I was brought up on the books of some thinkers whose names would be discovered by most of our fellow countrymen much later, during the perestroika years. Those books prompted me to reconsider again and again everything that had been shaped by religious education at home.

When I was fifteen, I left the home of my parents to join a geological party in Leningrad. Wishing to get a real taste of life and to put myself to the test, I also attended high school evening classes for factory and office workers. The books I had read before and the people I chanced to meet then helped me through the most dramatic and risky period of adolescence. . . .

Of course, I have doubts in life. If the ability to take a critical look at reality is lost—and this always involves doubting something—there emerges the risk of committing many mistakes.

—*"By Denying Divine Truth We Ruin the World"* (March 10, 2015)

The Church's Only Goal

121 The task of the Church has not changed in thousands of years, and we believe it will not change unto the end of the world. The Church is called to continue the ministry of our Lord Jesus Christ, bearing witness to divine truth and leading people to salvation. This is her only goal. The rest of what the Church does—be it social service, involvement in political dialogue, or mass media activities—is necessary only insofar as it can be used for bringing man to salvation.

—*Address to the participants of the 6th festival "Faith and Word"* (September 24, 2014)

A Co-Suffering Pastor

122 Once I had a very interesting conversation with a lady about a priest to whom she had gone to confession. She said, "When the priest was listening to my confession, I had a feeling that he was confessing together with me." It impressed the lady so much that she became a devout believer. In that ordinary pastor she saw someone who, instead of listening to her confession in a patronizing manner, was able to show understanding for her problems and spoke to her as a man who together *with* her was striving to escape from the burden of sin.

—*Address at the festival "Faith and Word"* (September 24, 2014)

True Heroism

123 Who is a strong person? It is someone who is able to defend his or her inner autonomy and freedom from destructive influence and temptation. The issue of personal integrity is closely related; the ability to resist temptation and be true to one's convictions is absolutely necessary if someone is to be a strong and free individual—one we might even call a hero. For without heroes, no society can exist.

—*"Experiments with Morality are Criminal," a speech at the Christmas Parliamentary Meetings of Russia's Council of the Federation* (January 28, 2014)

Traditional Values: "written in human hearts by God himself"

124 What do we mean by traditional values? These values are traditional and timeless: faith, love, duty, responsibility, and solidarity. These values have been present since the beginning of time; they weren't established by people and are therefore independent of any specific social circumstances. These are the standards implanted in human nature by God.

After all, no one is able to refute the idea of objective morality. The statement that morality has evolved over time in politics and culture is simply not true. "Thou shalt not kill" carries the same meaning for everyone, whether they are from Papua New Guinea, America, or Russia. If cultural evolution determined the moral nature of human beings, there would have been no universal human values at all, about which some people, including those of liberal outlook, like to talk so much. The very notion of universal human values draws our attention to the divine nature of morality. If man was created according to God's dispensation, then undermining moral foundations means destroying human personality. That is why I say that the moral law goes back neither to Christianity nor to Islam. It goes back to the time when human civilization was making its first steps; the moral law was written in human hearts by God himself.

—*"Experiments with Morality are Criminal"* (January 28, 2014)

The Spiritual Dimension of Culture

125 We are constantly choosing between true values and the surrogate values that masquerade as culture. Someone might object, saying, "Not everyone is able to listen to or read masterpieces all the time. After all, bad taste is not a sin. Why is the Church worrying about it?" I foresee such questions. Indeed, bad taste is not a sin, but in reality it can often lead to sin. That is why cultivation of good taste has, among other things, a spiritual dimension. Perhaps this is what Dostoyevsky meant when he said that beauty will save the world.

—*"Culture and Society: the View of the Church," a speech to the Patriarchal Council for Culture* (February 22, 2012)

Preserving Christian Civilization

126 Nowadays, the apostolic ministry of the Church has yet another very important dimension. All local Orthodox churches are called to bear common witness to Christ's truth in the face of the challenges of the modern world. Universal Orthodoxy needs to take on the task of preserving the uniqueness of Christian civilization in all its ethnic and cultural diversity. The tradition of the Church is rich enough to become the foundation for this joint effort.

—*Homily on the the Second Sunday after Pascha* (April 11, 2010)

A Guide and a Foundation

127 There is something special in the Christian faith, for it not only deals with theoretical truths in theology, but with things that affect our very life. The faith contains the truths that help keep us from going astray. In Greek, the word "sin" has, among other meanings, the meaning "to miss." Those committing sins miss the major target they are aiming at, and veer off the right course. The apostolic faith that has come to us from the incarnate Son of God enables us to hold this course.

The Lord is saving us through his grace and truth by renewing the covenant that people made with him in ancient times. He has given us a clear understanding of what is good and what is evil. The faith of the Church witnesses to this: what is true and what is false, what is sin and what is holiness. As a result, all of humanity still has—in spite of all our differences of opinions and variety of views and beliefs—the ability and an opportunity to preserve this foundation of human life through the Church.

—*Homily on the First Sunday of Lent* (February 21, 2010)

"You . . . have been brought near by the blood of Christ . . . who has made both one" (Eph 2.13–14)

128 The unity of the Church is sealed by the blood and passion of the Savior himself, as well as by the blood of martyrs and confessors. That is why it is vitally important to preserve this unity. Those who destroy this unity pound yet more nails into the body of Christ, repudiating the spiritual feats of preceding generations.

—*Homily on the feast of the Synaxis of the New Martyrs of Butovo* (May 1, 2010)

The Meaning of Apostolic Succession

129 What does succession mean? We say that the Church has preserved the apostolic succession of faith, grace, and sacramental life. Upholding Christ's faith, the Church at the same time undergoes different historical ordeals and acts in different circumstances.

Succession does not mean imitation. Just as there are no two identical people, there are no two identical epochs. Each epoch has its unique identity and its own problems. That is why, while preserving succession in the most important things, the Church has to respond to the questions raised by specific historical periods, trying to find the appropriate language and means to bring faith to people. The Church has to act vigorously in response to each era's specific historical situation, not dissolving because of its challenges, but preserving intact and strong the priceless tradition that was handed down to her at the dawn of her life.

—Homily on the anniversary of the repose of His Holiness Patriarch Alexy II (December 5, 2009)

The Church's Attitude toward the World

130 The Church is called to preserve and proclaim God's truth. She must not be involved in political struggles or turn the wrath of the masses on someone or something. . . . The only criterion the Church can use in her attitude to the world is the criterion of God's truth and nothing else. Neither political teachings, nor new-fangled transitory human ideas, nor political expediency must force the Church to make a judgment on the world, people, power structures, or society as a whole.

After all, the Church is not the one to judge. She only brings people to God's justice. "Judge not, that you be not judged" (Mt 7.1). The Church can only express her position on what is going on in the world with humility and in accordance with God's truth.

—*Homily on the feast of St Philip, Metropolitan of Moscow* (January 22, 2010)

"The victory that has overcome the world" (1 Jn 5.4)

131 In terrible years of tyranny and persecution, in the face of chaos and death—at all times the Church brings people the glad tidings that Christ is indeed risen. It is not the forces of sin and death but the love of God that triumphs in the ultimate victory. Such is the faith overcoming the whole world, as the holy apostle wrote: "Who is he who overcomes the world, but he who believes that Jesus is the Son of God?" (1 Jn 5.5).

—*"Truth and Hope," an article in* Rossiyskaya Gazeta (April 2, 2010)

"It all began when I was a boy"

132 It all began when I was a boy and would get into disputes over faith in God with my classmates. About a thousand pupils studied at my school at the time, I guess, and I was the only one not to wear a Pioneer's neckerchief (a red scarf worn by young communists in the Soviet Union). Everybody knew why I did not join the Pioneers: I was an ordinary boy who believed in God and at the same time had to study at a public school. Of course, my classmates, friends, and even teachers would ask me questions about God, faith, and the Church. Such notions as "catechesis," "apologetics," and "disputes over faith" became familiar to me much later, but what I tried to do as best as I could in my boyhood involved all of that. The polemics and conversations of that time aroused in me a feeling that I could devote my life to what I would now call "the interpretation of Christianity in the concepts understandable to people today."

—*Speech at the presentation of the book* A Pastor's Word *(November 17, 2004)*

A Combined Effort

133 The Savior commanded his disciples to live in complete unity with each other, and this commandment has not lost its importance. However, it is not given unto us to know the time when it will be fulfilled. What we have seen so far, as evidenced by various theological dialogues and tendencies revealing themselves in the Christian world today, is that the doctrinal unity of all Christians is not a possibility in the near future. Therefore, it seems to me that we need to redirect the thrust of our expectations, focusing on what really can unite us at the moment, that is, on demonstrating our commitment to the timeless values of the gospel and the apostolic tradition of the Church. Then we can combine our efforts for preaching these saving values to the modern world.

—*"The Orthodox Church and the Future of Inter-Christian Relations," a paper at the international meeting "People and Religions" (October 22, 2007)*

Inner Life and Involvement in Society

134 The Church says that she makes her pilgrimage in the world with the cross of the Savior in her hands. And what is a cross? It is an intersection of vertical and horizontal dimensions. The vertical dimension is man's inner life, his relationship with God. The horizontal dimension is man's involvement in the life of society. That is why we should never agree with individualistic moralists who say, "We are not interested in what is going on in society; the individual is our only concern."

At the same time, Christians today are often heard saying, "We only deal with social problems, while in private life people are free and can make their own decisions." Such things should not be said either. The Orthodox Church by no means speaks up against human freedom, but she calls upon people to mature in such a way that in their freedom, they conform to the moral responsibility that man has before God.

—*Interview with Ukrainian journalists* (July 15, 2010)

Dialogue and Joint Efforts

135 All of the major problems of the modern world can be solved through dialogue and joint efforts. The Russian Orthodox Church agrees entirely with such an approach, relying on holy Scripture, which says, "Have regard for good things in the sight of all men. If it is possible, as much as depends on you, live peaceably with all men" (Rom 12.17–18). That is why it is important to promote cooperation among people of different views and beliefs at every level of the human community, be it in the family or at work, in the village or in the city. Can we imagine a happy family if the members act at cross-purposes? The only way to solve common problems is through dialogue, providing mutual support, and acting in accord with each other. If the dialogue proves to be efficacious at the level of family and at work, it can help at the global level as well.

—*Speech at a meeting with the public in Kazakhstan*
  (January 17, 2010)

Becoming Like God

136 It is impossible to reach union with God without being like him. The ancient philosophers, who were heathens, would fairly say that like is known by like. You cannot reach communion with God if you are totally unlike him, because God just cannot be with the one who is unlike him. That is why salvation comes through the cross. It does not come through human wisdom, the power of knowledge, political power, or the organization of society, but through the cross of Christ in which and through which the saving love of God was revealed in full measure.

—*Homily on the feast of the Exaltation of the Holy Cross* (September 27, 2009)

"Liturgical services are my life"

137 Liturgical services are my life. When I hold services I even feel better physically, because during prayer a certain balance of inner forces is reached. It is hard to speak of yourself; it is harder to speak of your innermost life. It is even harder to speak of such things for the press, because they are more suitable for conversation with your spiritual father. And yet I wish to say that my life's work is serving God, and in the heart of this work is serving the Divine Liturgy. Anything else is secondary.

—*"The Light of the Good," an interview with* Rossiyskaya Gazeta (January 23, 2009)

How do we recognize Christ?

138 Why did none of those who served in the temple recognize the divine infant Jesus when they met him? Only St Simeon, the God-receiver, recognized him. Why so? Simeon had prepared himself for that meeting. If we also prepare ourselves for meeting the

Lord by softening our hearts, training our minds in God's word, and heightening our feelings, then meeting God will always cause our hearts to leap with joy, tears of tenderness to run from our eyes, and the deepest spiritual feelings to well up inside us. . . . Our faith is based on this joyous experience of meeting God. We do not need any more logical arguments, because touching Christ, with joy and trembling, in our faith and in our hope, provides proof of the real presence of God in our life.

—*Homily on the Meeting of the Lord* (February 15, 2001)

"Blessed are the merciful, for they shall obtain mercy" (Mt 5.7)

139 Reflecting on the parable of the rich man and Lazarus, St Cyprian of Carthage said the words that afterwards were also repeated by St Basil. These words help us understand what is necessary for our prayers to be heard by God: If we do not hear the entreaties of the poor, then we do not deserve to have our prayers heard by God.[7] What marvelous, striking words! They correlate with the golden rule: "Therefore, whatever you want men to do to you, do also to them" (Mt 7.12). One can paraphrase these words in this way: Whatever you wish that the Lord would do to you, do also to other people.

This is so because the Lord reveals himself to us in our neighbors. If we are indifferent to the sorrow of other people, if our heart is deaf and does not respond to their sorrow and needs, then our prayers and our crying will be in vain. We will be shedding

---

[7]Cyprian, *On the Lord's Prayer* 33: "He promises that he will be present and says that he hears and protects those who loosen the knots of unrighteousness [cf. Is 58.6] from their hearts, and who give alms to the servants of God, and act in accordance with his direction. Those who hear what God demands should be done will themselves merit a hearing from God." *On the Lord's Prayer: Tertullian, Cyprian, and Origen*, Alistair Stewart-Sykes, trans. (Crestwood, NY: St Vladimir's Seminary Press, 2004), 90.

selfish crocodile tears, which will not be pleasing to God. Our prayers ought to be coupled with help for and love of our neighbors. When we do this, we will join Lazarus in the bosom of Abraham, and the Lord will hear our sighs.

The mystery of spiritual life is based on this necessary relationship, so well expressed by St Cyprian: There can be neither prayer nor hope for salvation without works, because faith, if it has no works, is dead (Jas 2.17, 20).

—*Homily on the feast of the Joy of All Who Sorrow Icon of the Mother of God* (November 6, 2011)

"We should approach the holy chalice as often as we can"

140 The Lord came into the world in order to save us from the tempting power of evil, the dominion of sin, the triumph of falsehood and hypocrisy, and from captivity to the devil. Are we able to resist this diabolic power? Weak and infirm, we easily submit to temptations and embark on the path of sin—and how infinitely difficult it is to embark on the path of salvation! Each of us knows this from his own experience.

Many have probably pledged to themselves: "I will free myself from this sin, I will try not to do this," only to fall again into weakness and sin. How are we to find salvation in our infirmity? It is through our belief and firm conviction that the Lord has brought us salvation. Through his sacrifice, his great deed, his death, and his resurrection, we are saved, for through the sacrifice of Jesus Christ the power of God is revealed to us.

We draw upon this power in the mystery of the holy Eucharist. Each person who receives the body and blood of the Savior truly partakes of the divine life, receives forgiveness of sins, and inherits life everlasting. That is why we should approach the holy chalice as often as we can.

—*Homily for Great and Holy Thursday* (April 20, 2006)

"Speaking to all those who are ready to hear"

141 I suppose in each era there arises within the Church a certain false notion of whom we should talk to and whom we should not talk to. So too in our day some have the idea that under no circumstances should we talk to representatives of other Christian confessions and various faiths. As once the apostle Peter was told, we too are now warned: "Speak to no one apart from the faithful!"

Yet as the Equals-to-the-Apostles Cyril and Methodius went to the infidel Khazars and to the pagan Slavs (our distant ancestors whom the ancient Byzantines called "Russians," who lived in the south of today's Russia and Ukraine), and to Moravia and the Slav homelands, meeting with the infidels and pagans and preaching the word of God to them in their native language, so too all in the Church of Christ are called to tread the apostolic path in speaking to all those who are ready to hear. We are to bear to all those whom we encounter the witness that we are called to give to others as we imitate the feat of the apostles, the feat of Sts Cyril and Methodius.

—*Homily on the feast of Sts Cyril and Methodius* (May 24, 2016)

"Waiting for the risen Savior"

142 Our most precious experience is waiting for the risen Savior. This waiting does not have to be restricted to the Parousia, his second and dreadful coming. Instead, we have to wait for the Lord at every moment of our life, because each person, passing from this life to life eternal, will see Christ and give an account of his or her earthly life at its end. So will all humanity and the entire world give an account of their history to the Son of God when he, according to the angels' words (cf. Acts 1.11), comes from heaven for the last judgment of the human race. . . .

We are given the time between the coming of the Savior into the world and his second and dreadful coming to create, to struggle, to fight evil, and to maintain divine truth and righteousness in our lives and in the life of the world around us. We are called not to an indifferent waiting for the Savior, but to the accomplishment of his will to great effect.

—*Homily on the feast of the Ascension of the Lord* (May 28, 2009)

The Source of the Martyrs' Strength

143 When you read the ancient texts describing the spiritual feats of the holy martyrs, both men and women, you involuntarily ask about the source of their power and strength. How could a young girl endure what was beyond the strength of the physically strongest and most courageous people? Then one begins to understand that no physical power or human will is capable of giving such patience to a human being, for it was the will and the power of God that supported . . . all the martyrs.

What was said is very instructive for modern people, many of whom wish to be strong without fail. It is a very good desire, but one should remember that the true power is the power of the human spirit. Without God, this power is concealed from man, and then he can rely only on his own resources and strength, which are incommensurate with the power of God. It is impossible to achieve on one's own the power that the holy martyrs possessed. Those who desire the strength to win and to achieve much in their lives should remember that all these human victories are possible when we have a strong spirit impregnated with the power of God.

—*Homily on the feast of St Barbara* (December 17, 2010)

St Catherine: An Example for Today's Christians

144 The life of the holy great martyr Catherine is a great example for us. Indeed, today's life so often lures us by various temptations of money, power, elevated positions, or the acquisition of new material goods in order to give us a sense of advantage and prestige. We are also tempted to compromise our faith as we attempt to reconcile it with temptation. How many are these temptations!

St Catherine, however, remained a secret Christian while smiling to the heathen emperor. She did not live in a poor family but in the family of a rich man, an emperor's governor, yet the wealth she was surrounded with did not prevent her from having a real experience of communion with God. When the question arose as to where her heart was committed, she answered bravely and truthfully.

Christ told us, "For where your treasure is, there your heart will be also" (Mt 6.21). St Catherine's treasure was the Lord, not the wealth that surrounded her. Therefore God himself gave her a great power: the power of spirit. That is why we remember in our twenty-first century the holy great martyr Catherine as a genius of spirit, as a great heroine, and as a God-pleasing saint.

—*Homily on the feast of St Catherine* (December 7, 2010).

Transforming the World from the Perspective of the Kingdom

145 It is not until we acquire spiritual sight that we can understand where we are going and can find the right way, because human life becomes meaningful only when seen from the perspective of eternity. When we see and sense the glory of the eighth day[8]

---

[8]The fathers speak of the "eighth day" as a type of eternity (standing outside the cycle of the seven-day week). "For, Scripture knows as a day without

and that of the divine kingdom—which is not only to come at the end of time, but is present within this world already—when we realize the necessity of subjecting our earthly life to God's law and his commandments, then our human efforts, with the assistance of God's grace, will transfigure our sinful world by drawing it closer to the unending divine kingdom. . . . The Church is called to exert such an effect on society that will transform this society in accordance with God's law and thus will make the earthly, created world reflect God's grace in full measure. Just as there is no other purpose for the Church but that of transforming this world, so is there no other purpose for man but that of entering the kingdom of God, through first seeing this kingdom and then conforming to its laws.

—*Homily on the feast of the Transfiguration of the Lord* (August 19, 2009)

An Intellectual Message from the Church

146 The voice of the Church must be a clarion call and not noise. If we become indistinguishable from the noise around us, then people begin to regard our words as indifferently as they would regard anything else. This is the reason that an intellectual message from the Church contributes greatly to the people's enlightenment. And it goes without saying that only those who couple their talents with hard work are able to fuel an intellectual spark.

—*Speech to the faculty and students of the Moscow Theological Schools* (December 14, 2008)

evening, without succession, and without end, that day which the psalmist called the eighth, because it lies outside this week of time. Therefore, whether you say 'day' or 'age' you will express the same idea." St Basil the Great, *Hexameron* 2.8. *Saint Basil: Exegetic Homilies*, The Fathers of the Church, vol. 46, Agnes Clare Way, trans. (Washington, D.C.: The Catholic University of America, 1963), 35.—*Ed.*

Love and Sacrifice

147 Love is always linked to sacrifice. Where love is, there too is the capacity to sacrifice oneself, and where love is not, there can be no sacrifice. Our Lord Jesus Christ came into the world and sacrificed himself for people. This is the image by which the good husband surrenders himself to his wife, gives of himself through his time, his means and much else, while the good wife sacrifices her time and well-being, and on occasion even her health for her husband, and she surrenders all her strength for the sake of her family. We are good to each other when we give rather than strive to receive. The ability to give is a testimony to love.

—*Speech at the Patriarchal Awards Ceremony to members of the organizational committee of the All-Russian Day of the Family, Love, and Fidelity* (November 14, 2008)

The American Church and the Russian Church

148 The American Church arose as a result of the missionary labors of the Russian Orthodox Church, first of all through the monks of Valaam monastery, who almost 220 years ago set foot on the Aleutian islands off the coast of Alaska and began an Orthodox mission there. We especially recall today St Herman of Alaska, a monk of Valaam. We recall also St Innocent, metropolitan of Moscow, who was born in Siberia and dedicated almost all his life to mission efforts among the peoples of eastern Siberia, the far north, and Alaska. We especially recall also today St Tikhon, Patriarch of Moscow, who for many years served on the American continent and did much for the establishment and growth of the diocese of our church in America, heralding the beginning of organized church life for Orthodox people on the continent of North America. . . .

The Orthodox faith is a very important factor as we endeavor to maintain good relations between Russia and the United States of America. All other factors are transient: at one point they are positive, at another point in history they are viewed as negative. In one period pragmatic good relations between countries are established, while at another moment these good relations are destroyed. This is typical of the external world that does not live according to God's law.

True friendship between people and good relations can be established only at the level of the human heart. The Orthodox churches in America and the Russian Orthodox Church are the real bridge that is capable of uniting the hearts of the Russian and American peoples. And although the Orthodox Church in the United States is not as large in numbers of the faithful, she has a completely special spiritual mission, since she is a daughter church of the Russian Orthodox Church. We are connected in true fraternal relationship with the American people.

—*Homily on the Feast of the Presentation of the Mother of God in the Temple* (December 4, 2014)

The Mission of the American Orthodox Church

149 We should preserve [the historical relationship between the Russian Church and the Orthodox Church in America] as a treasure, as something that is from history, the past—especially today, when the relations between our countries have worsened drastically. The task of our churches is to pray and work in order that the Lord would grant his mercy to the peoples of our countries, so that, by God's power, a healthy moral foundation—which originates in God's biblical morals—would once again be fortified, and so that the relations between our countries would strengthen, based on common moral values.

That is why we endure deviations from God's moral standards so painfully. These deviations take place both in the United States and in other western countries at the present time. It is a great challenge for Christian churches. Many of them, especially Protestant organizations, fail to overcome this challenge—they follow the path of renouncing their own identity, and refuse the moral values of the gospel in favor of political fashion. But the Orthodox Church cannot do this, and therefore the Orthodox Church encourages people to profess the faith. We have a right to speak about it like this here at this cathedral, because our church has gone through decades of suffering and confession, but it has not faltered or compromised its integrity.

That is why we heartily wish that the Orthodox Church in America would preserve fidelity to Christ, his commandments, and would be, if not very bright and strong, nevertheless still a light for its people. We are aware that even the light of a small candle becomes a powerful point of reference and helps people find their way to salvation.

—*Homily on the Feast of the Presentation of the Mother of God in the Temple* (December 4, 2014)

The Legacy of St Tikhon

150 Patriarch Tikhon was a true peacemaker. This, of course, flowed not from any personal qualities, but from the words of the apostle Paul that we heard today in the Divine Liturgy: Christ is our peace and has gathered together the divided (Eph 2.14). . . .

Which of St Tikhon's legacies are we to keep? In new conditions we are to continue his ministry of reconciliation. Today various historical, cultural, and philosophical views hold sway. Often people, as they clash in a serious struggle, draw the Church too into this struggle and pose the question: who are you with—the right or the left, with this group of individuals or with that? Our answer is the same as that given by St Tikhon—we are with *our people*, because the Church bears the great responsibility of preserving the unity of our people. For Christ is our peace and he can reconcile those who are irreconcilable, he can unite the divided, he can bring peace to the most restless of souls. . . . In continuing Patriarch Tikhon's witness, we shall always say with the apostle Paul: Christ is our peace (Eph 2.14).

—*Homily on the anniversary of St Tikhon's election to the patriarchal throne* (November 18, 2012)

Moral Consensus: A Foundation for Civilization

151 All of us have to reflect upon the ways in which human civilization has developed. All of us have to reflect upon how scientific and technological or, as we say now, post-industrial society is to be joined to those spiritual and religious values without which a human being cannot live. The Church can be harassed and pushed to one side, and people can be deprived of the chance of satisfying their religious needs, but it is impossible to kill religious sentiments, and we all know this very well. We have to harness human freedom to moral responsibility. We have to give every person the chance to live in accordance with God's law. We must not limit the expression of religious sentiments and simultaneously we must not limit human freedom of choice. If we unite all of these component parts, then we will build a viable civilization.

And if we cannot do this, then we are condemned to permanent struggle and permanent suffering. We cannot build the future through a tug-of-war, the victory of one model over another, or through the creation of artificial forms of living together that accord neither with our moral nature nor religious sentiment. And if humanity attains moral consensus, and if this moral consensus becomes a part of international law, then there is a chance that we can build a just global system of civilization.

—*Interview on Nativity for the TV channel* Russia-1 (January 7, 2016)

How to Grow in Faith

152 What is faith? It is the means of constant self-control and the influencing of one's soul and consciousness. When we pray in the morning and the evening, we ought to subject ourselves to a rigorous analysis. I know that sometimes it is difficult for people to read the prayers, because Church Slavonic is not so easy to grasp, and also there is not enough time. Yet there is enough time to think about ourselves and to reflect upon our lives and the past day. So do this before the face of God! Subject your actions to analysis, control them, and ask God for forgiveness and enlightenment so that we do not repeat these mistakes. If we have spoken wrongly to someone, raised our voices, corrected someone sharply, cause them pain or offense, or deceived them . . . we can tell all of this to God and ask for his help. Then we will transform ourselves and we will transform our inner world. We will become stronger! It is on this inner spiritual strength that our well-being depends—in my view, to a far greater degree than any external material factors.

—*Interview on Nativity for the TV channel* Russia-1 (January 7, 2016)

Prayer and our Relationship with God

153 We have already spoken of how it is good, each morning and each evening as we stand before God, to analyze our lives, to repent, and to act in accordance with this analysis in the future. Now I would like to say something in general about prayer.

Prayer is a completely special thing; God, indeed, did make us autonomous, and also autonomous in relation to him. He gave us such freedom that we can believe in him or not believe in him, live according to his law or not, turn to him or not turn to him. Of course, if we turn away from him, we will live merely according to the laws and ways of this world. There are the laws of physics—this is what we will live by, or else we create our own laws and live by them. Yet prayer is a way out of this autonomy. We say: "This is how you have made me, and I want to be with you." Prayer is the means of inviting God into one's own life. Through prayer we make God our co-worker.

—*Interview on Nativity for the TV channel* Russia-1 (January 7, 2016)

"Good increases good"

154 Our lives become pleasing to God when we simply accomplish good deeds. Many people are in need of these good deeds, from our kin with whom we live to those we encounter at work and in the various circumstances of life. If we learn to accomplish good, then we become happy people, for good increases good.

—*Interview on Nativity for the TV channel* Russia-1 (January 7, 2016)

The Russian Church's Rebirth

155 If people did not gather in the temples of God, then nobody would have built them, nobody would have restored them, and the terrible epoch of the destruction of holy sites in Russia would not have passed by so quickly as it has in our time. The spiritual rebirth of our motherland is a phenomenon that has no analogy in history, and this means that we are witnesses to a completely special era. We live at a special time when—literally—from non-being, from destruction, and from defilement, the Russian

Orthodox Church has been reborn, and people once more have the opportunity to pray to God.

Today, church life is proceeding well. We are restoring old churches and building new ones, we are setting up Sunday Schools and other educational institutions for children, social ministry is growing, and the Church is engaged with the young without hindrance and is accomplishing many other socially important and beneficial things. And let's not forget that the most important event of all is taking place as we celebrate the divine Eucharist and offer prayers to God.

At the same time, while rejoicing in what we are experiencing, we must not forget the past; the faith, indeed, did not simply emerge from nowhere. Our faith has been transmitted to us by our forefathers, our parents and grandparents, who in difficult times of persecution baptized their grandchildren and kept the Orthodox faith while even keeping this secret from their own children.

—*Homily after a Prayer Service in St Michael's Church of the Trinity Monastery in Birsk* (June 4, 2016)

The Persecution of Christians in the Middle East

156 What is happening in the Middle East, the birthplace of Christianity, is a tragedy. Today, as a result of military action and the actions of terrorists, we observe a dramatic reduction in the Christian population. We are, of course, speaking of using the joint efforts of the churches of East and West and mobilizing all people who can do something positive to halt this process. We have to preserve the Christian presence in the Middle East and North Africa.

—*Interview on the TV channel RT* (February 16, 2016)

How to Defeat Terrorism

157 In order for us to defeat terrorism, all of us have to become different people. Terrorism is in the first place a philosophical challenge. We have to understand what is happening to people who take up arms in order to fight for God. I firmly believe that the new development in human civilization, which has resulted in the renunciation of God and divine moral law, has provoked the appearance of terrorism.

We have to reach a common global moral consensus. On what foundation can people live together, other than the foundation of certain common values? And how can we reach common values when there are various political parties, various philosophical systems, and various religious systems? How can we achieve a consensus on a global scale? Only by one means: the basis of our consensus must be the moral sense of the human person. That moral sense and moral nature has been embedded in the human soul by God. Moral concepts are the same for me as a Russian as they are for you as an American. Indeed, if we go to Papua New Guinea, we see that there too in the depths of the human soul are the same moral concepts.

We should not undermine this moral sense by introducing laws aimed at the destruction of traditional morality; instead, we must agree upon these common moral values and on the basis of this consensus build a common global civilization. In this civiliza-tion there would be no place for terrorism. If someone tried to manipulate people in order to cause harm to others, it would be very difficult for that person to succeed, for that appeal would go against the common understanding of good and evil. We should all together try to build a new civilization on the basis of a com-mon moral consensus. I believe that this is possible.

—Interview on the TV channel RT (February 16, 2016)

Reason, Faith, and Miracles

158 Our contemporaries are all too willing to believe in the unconditional primacy of rational knowledge over all other forms. However, even our everyday existence convinces us that life is far greater, broader, and deeper than our understanding of it. We encounter miracles in Scripture and in the lives of the saints, and these do not fit into the framework of rational analysis. Otherwise, they would not be miracles! By means of miracles, God demonstrates the limited nature of material existence: a miracle is different from an ordinary event in that in a miracle, the natural order is vanquished and through the power of God natural laws are overcome.

However, the meaning of miracles does not lie merely in the fact that the laws of nature have been overthrown, but in the affirmation of the human person's closeness to God. All things are possible for him who is the first Lawgiver. . . . A miracle demands not analysis but faith. Where faith falters, where inspiration has died—here a miracle can help people to be strengthened in their faith. At the same time, a miracle can only *invite* faith, it cannot compel. . . . There always remains the possibility that the inquiring mind will resist the miracle and seek out a natural cause for it. Ultimately, one with genuine and deep faith does not seek miracles: he first of all seeks God and entrusts himself and all his life completely to him.

—*"Patriarch Kirill: The main miracle of St Sergius is the person of St Sergius himself," an interview for the journal* Expert (July 21, 2014)

St Sergius of Radonezh

159 The main miracle of St Sergius is the person of St Sergius himself. He was a man who abandoned the world and became the center of Rus'. He avoided all authority, both secular and ecclesiastical, and yet he became an absolute authority in the state and Church. Consciously choosing a place unsuited for a normal life to engage in his spiritual endeavors, he founded a huge monastery and the town of Sergiev Posad. A humble monk, he mobilized and inspired the Russian people in defense of the fatherland.

—*"The main miracle of St Sergius,"* Expert (July 21, 2014)

"My grandfather's stories . . . formed my outlook on life"

160 In general, the duty of parents and the older generation is to form the outlook of people and their view of life. In this sense my grandfather, who had endured many trials and by a miracle remained alive, played a special role. He should not have continued living as he endured the terrible afflictions of the Solovki labor camp in the distant north, in the cold White Sea.

He left a powerful and bright trace in my soul. I would listen to his stories attentively and, still being a child, I was struck by how calmly he would speak of his unimaginable sufferings. He always emphasized that without God's help he not only would never have become a priest, but he would not have remained alive.

And my grandfather's stories, of course, formed my outlook on life. They shaped my understanding that faith is a great power, and it is always a gift of God for which one may even give up one's life. My grandfather was always ready to endure these sufferings—and not only him, but also his generation of Orthodox Christians.

—*Homily after a Prayer Service in St Michael's Church of the Trinity Monastery in Birsk* (June 4, 2016)

Openness to the World

161 It is important for us to understand that in our hearts there should not be pride and pharisaical condemnation of all those who are different from us, but sincere love and the desire that all those who by God's will are around us be saved. Where there is no love, where the desire merely to declare one's superiority over others holds sway, there can be neither God's truth nor genuine zeal for Christ's Church. We cannot cut ourselves off with a wall from those for whom God ascended the cross, whether me or you or the whole world. As the evangelist says, "For God so loved the world that he gave his only-begotten Son, that whoever believes in him should not perish, but have everlasting life" (Jn 3.16).

If God loves this world, then we too must be open to the whole world, to every person who is ready to hear our word, regardless of his or her religion. We are to follow the example of the apostle and become all things to all men, so that some may be saved (1 Cor 9.22). And this means to hold dialogue—thoughtfully, critically, and with principle answering all manner of questions without becoming enclosed within oneself or choosing the easy road of talking only to those with whom we agree. How else are we going to bring the apostolic witness to the whole world? The Church will never renounce this mission; that would be to betray Christ. Without the humble and patient readiness for dialogue, we will not only not bring the light of Christ to the world, but we will also no longer be able to preserve the unity of the Orthodox faith, for in the worldwide Orthodox family complete agreement does not always and in all things hold sway.

—*Speech at the celebrations in honor of the 70th anniversary of the Department for External Church Relations of the Moscow Patriarchate (May 19, 2016)*

"Redeeming the time" (Col 4.5)

162 The Church's endeavors to communicate with the external world are an integral part of Orthodox mission. This mission is not always the direct preaching of the word of God; however, it helps millions of people to see Orthodoxy with new eyes, helping them feel the beauty and power of Orthodoxy. This is achieved through a kind word, good deeds, and attending to the needs of people: in other words, through the example of our lives. As the apostle Paul says: "Walk in wisdom toward those who are outside, redeeming the time. Let your speech always be with grace, seasoned with salt, that you may know how you ought to answer each one" (Col 4.5–6).

—*Speech for the 70th anniversary of the DECR of the MP*
  (May 19, 2016)

The Cross: "a stumbling block to some and foolishness to others"

163 Why did God choose self-humiliation, which is madness in the eyes of every sane man? Why did he choose such a way of salvation? For one purpose only, which was so that everyone could see that it is God who saves man. Neither human wisdom nor human power has anything to do with it. . . . The preaching of the cross shows that God refused to resort to any human force at all in his mission of salvation. The Lord chose the cross, a symbol of humiliation, weakness and defeat—a stumbling block to some and foolishness to others (cf. 1 Cor 1.23)—in order to bring salvation to the whole world from this cross.

—*Homily on the feast of the Exaltation of the Holy Cross* (September 27, 2014)

The Bishop's Task in the Modern World

164 The ministry of a bishop is primarily the great mission of testifying to the light that has come into the world, the true light that cannot be overcome by any darkness. In our time a great number of people follow various paths through life, not knowing where they are going and why. Drifting wearily in search of illusory pleasures, guided by destructive ideas, they find it hard to distinguish between good and evil and become entangled in falsehood. Many today go down wicked paths under the influence of the propaganda of sin and moral permissiveness. We, as Christ's ministers, do all that is possible so that faith is born and strengthened in people's hearts, so that love for the Savior is kindled. The founder calls upon his Church to proclaim the gospel of the kingdom and to preach the truth. This is why we cannot enclose ourselves within our communities, concentrating solely on internal affairs, when the world around us lies in evil and when spiritual blindness stops the eyes of those that are near and that are far off.

The Lord turns to his disciples and calls upon them: ". . . lift up your eyes and look at the fields, for they are already white for harvest!" (Jn 4.35) In spite of the huge number of temptations, the secularization of public life, and the re-evaluation of basic, fundamental moral values, many people today are striving to find the true meaning of life and to find their way to God. Their hearts and minds thirst after truth. In order that the good news reach them, the voice of the Church must resound clearly and convincingly, testifying to the one who was "delivered up because of our offenses, and was raised because of our justification" (Rom 4.25). We have to try to find words that each can understand when addressing either the individual or a group of people in a language that means something to them.

*—Homily at the presentation of the bishop's staff to Bp John of
Jelgava, auxiliary of the diocese of Riga* (March 27, 2016)

Finding Meaning and Strength in Afflictions

165 In Scripture and in the fathers of the Church, we encounter an assertion that often provokes a negative reaction in modern-day people: those whom the Lord loves he chastises (Prov 3.12). If the Lord visits us with afflictions, this means that he has not turned away from us, but has given us the chance to overcome difficulties and to grow. It is this approach toward our afflictions and sorrows that imparts to the Christian great spiritual power, helping him transcend his difficult circumstances and not lose his head and direction in life, or fall beneath the weight of burdens.

—*Homily on the eve of the First Sunday of Lent* (March 19, 2016)

Human Strength and the Narrow Path

166 To be a believer has always meant to be a strong person. In Soviet times, we were told that religion was the province of the weak, but I could never consent to this, for I could always see before me the example of the martyrs and confessors of our Church, and of those with whom I studied and worked. It was clear that in order to pass beneath these vaults you had to be a strong person, and at that time to be especially strong and go against the general current.

Yet, in a certain sense, the Christian has always gone against the common current. The Lord calls us to go down the narrow and not the wide path. The wide path is easy, and as we move along it, we don't have to be the captain of the vessel; the steering is done for us and we are taken along. But when one goes down the narrow path, then one always defines one's direction and trajectory. The narrow path is always difficult; however, it is this path which leads us, as the gospel says, to the kingdom of God and to victory in our earthly life. There are no easy paths upon which a human being can travel if he hopes to achieve significant results, whether in his professional or personal life. It is especially important for us who have devoted ourselves to service in the Church to understand that if we travel on the easy path, it will be impossible to achieve success in the great and saving cause of ministry to the Lord and his holy Church. . . .

And in order to preserve this inner strength and be capable of going along the narrow path, we have to rely upon God's help. Human strength is weaker than the power of the devil, but divine power transcends all human and diabolic power, and if through prayer and faith we call down upon ourselves the power of God, then we become strong and able to travel the narrow path toward the kingdom of God.

—*Homily at Matins for the Saturday of the Akathist* (April 15, 2016)

"I was in prison and you came to me" (Mt 25.36)

167 Intercession for prisoners has always been a part of the mission of the Orthodox Church. It speaks to the very nature of the Church, since concern for the salvation of sinners is what is at the center of church ministry. Prison brings together people who all have one thing in common—they have all sinned; they have all committed transgressions, including those that in earthly life are violations of the law. And it is here in this earthly life that they suffer punishment for their infringements of the law, for their sins according to the legislature are considered to be crimes, that is, the violation of the norms of life in society.

A prison term is a trial for the human person. Nobody emerges from prison the same as they went in. It is a great challenge for a person's soul. Yet, at the same time, it is a great opportunity given by God. Prison can break and cripple a person or plunge him into the depths of despair, but it can also transform him and generate within him new life.

And the Church goes into prisons so that prisoners do not go along the former, destructive path. The main goal of the Church in the prison cell is to help each inmate to encounter Christ.

—*Speech at the opening of a session of the Higher Church Council* (April 13, 2016)

"An effort to transfigure this world"

168 To be a Christian has always suggested an effort to transfigure this world, to enhance the moral atmosphere of society, and to draw Christ to those who do not know Him. Thanks to the work of the apostles who witnessed the transfiguration of the Lord, the gospel was proclaimed in many countries. Many generations of saints took the apostles as a pattern and labored everywhere on earth so that the ideal revealed at the transfiguration might be realized in ever-changing circumstances.

As Christians, we also ought to follow their example, because the world—which underwent many crises in the previous century—forgot Christ and turned away from him, and so continues to lie in wickedness (cf. 1 John 5.19), needing to be transfigured by God's power, as well as by our work.

—*"The Transfiguration of the Lord," a message to the readers of* Pravoslavnaya Beseda (2009)

"How can we love our neighbor?"

169 Each of us, knowing that the greatest of God's commandments is the commandment to love our neighbor (Mt 22.39), has more than likely asked himself the question: "What does this commandment mean? How can we love our neighbor? We even lack love for those closest to us, so what can we say of those who are not linked to us through blood or the ties of friendship? How can we love these people?"

This question is always in the mind of the believer as he hears the call: "Bear one another's burdens, and so fulfill the law of Christ" (Gal 6.2). He who consciously and responsibly relates to the word of God and perceives this word as addressed to him personally cannot dismiss the words: "Bear one another's burdens, and so fulfill the law of Christ." As he examines his own life and the condition of his heart and mind, he realizes that he does not love other people. At best, he is indifferent or maybe polite and of a good disposition, but where is love to be found here?

Perhaps this commandment surpasses human capabilities? Perhaps by our very nature we cannot fulfill it? But this simply cannot be so. The Lord did not lay upon us burdens that we are unable to bear (Mt 23.4), for he himself said: "My yoke is easy, and my burden is light" (Mt 11.30). This means that we can observe the commandment to love each other without difficulty.

In today's epistle reading (2 Jn 1.1–13) we find an answer to this question. Love consists of walking in God's commandments. We do not have to summon up emotional strength, we don't have to become hysterical, we should not become sentimental, we should not wring our hands, we should not do that which goes against our inner state, we should not force ourselves to love—no power can ever force us! Fulfill God's commandments. The fulfillment of God's commandments, which are so simple, is what reveals the mystery of love of our neighbor.

—*Homily on the 15th anniversary of the discovery of the relics of St Matrona of Moscow* (March 8, 2013)

Heroic Acts

170 We must learn how to accomplish deeds that appear to go against the general current of life. . . . The ability to accomplish heroic acts, to sacrifice oneself or that which is dear to oneself, or what we have saved up for many years in laboring for higher goals; the ability to give one's life for others, as the Lord calls us to do; the ability to dedicate all our life to God in renouncing the many values of this world—all of these acts surpass human reason and acquire the greatest value in the eyes of God. God is never indebted to us—we are forever in his debt. And if we do something for his sake, especially if we manifest concern for those who need it, such as the sick, the unfortunate, the orphans, the elderly and the aged, and the lonely, then the Lord will incline his mercy toward us.

—*Homily on the eve of Great and Holy Wednesday* (April 30, 2013)

The Importance of Repentance

171 Why does Christ's mission begin with repentance? It begins this way for this reason alone: that repentance is something greatly important for the human person.

Today, mention of repentance often evokes a negative reaction in people. Some imagine it to be endlessly dreary. Others think of repentance in a legal way: someone voluntarily gives evidence against himself when circumstances in life or fear oblige him to make a guilty plea.

However, the fact that the Lord began his ministry with the preaching of repentance testifies to the special significance of repentance in the life of the human person. We may say that repentance is a fundamental religious truth, an extremely essential dimension of our spiritual life, without which the fullness of human existence would remain unattainable. . . . Repentance presupposes in the first instance the inner re-evaluation of oneself, a critical self-analysis, and the ability to look at oneself from the outside, to condemn our own sins, and submit to God's judgment and mercy.

—*A Pastor's Word* (Moscow: DECR, 2008), 113–114

Exiles from Paradise

172 The expulsion from paradise is primarily the image of God's rejection and abandonment of the human person. The human person abandoned by God is alone with himself, cut off from communion with God. The human person recedes from a life with God and in God, separated from the fount of everlasting grace by an insuperable barrier. This happens not because of the Maker's ill will, for God in his nature is the all-beneficent Giver of good things and mercy. The reason he is abandoned by God lies in the human person's own falling away from him, in his refusal to be with God all the days of his life. To experience a life in communion with God, one must first of all observe the law that God offers for salvation.

—*Homily on Cheesefare Sunday* (March 17, 2002)

"Prayer and repentance are a single action"

173 "O Trinity above all essence and worshiped as one God, take from me the heavy burden of sin, and since thou art compassionate grant me tears of repentance."[9] These few words contain the entire essence of what occurs in the human soul at the moment of true repentance and reconciliation with God. It is impossible to free oneself from the heavy burden of sin purely by summoning up our spiritual and physical strength with our human powers. . . . If we believe that we are capable of managing our inner spiritual life independently, that we have no need of any help in perfecting ourselves, then we are greatly mistaken. This has not been given to us! Only the "Trinity above all essence and worshiped as one God" can deliver us from the heavy burden of sin, and only the merciful God can reduce our transgressions to ashes, cleanse our souls, and grant us hope in salvation.

[9]The Great Penitential Canon of St Andrew of Crete, Ode 1.

This purification happens in response to our efforts, which are in response to God's grace. In being aware of our sin, we ought not only repent of it with a contrite heart, but also ask God to free us from the burden of sin. This is why prayer and repentance are a single action: neither repentance without prayer nor prayer without repentance is capable of transforming our lives.

—*Homily on Wednesday of the First Week of Great Lent*
(February 21, 2007)

"A real, true human being"

174 Christ is the tuning fork of humanity. . . . If we lose his example, we will have nothing with which to confront the powerful challenges of our day, which are aimed primarily at undermining the traditional and true notion of the human person. It is extremely important that we look deeply into the image of Christ and measure our thoughts and actions by him. We are to be inspired by the example of his boundless love toward people, his zeal in prayer and ministry to God, his modesty and humility, his intolerance of sin and great patience toward sinners, his courage in enduring the afflictions and burdens of earthly life, his openness and simplicity in speaking with others, and his infinite giving that was manifested in all things. God comes into this world not as a powerful and glorious king so that all may serve and please him; he is born in the humble surroundings of a cave for cattle in order to minister to people and give his life up for their salvation.

For the first time in history God demonstrated to the whole world what a real, true human being should be like. He not only revealed this but also granted all things necessary so that all who believe in him could become such a human being.

—*Address to TV viewers on Nativity* (January 7, 2014)

The Ultimate Authority

175 For the Church, the ultimate authority is Christ himself. She can and must cooperate with the surrounding world. Under no circumstances, however, can she bow her head before any authority if it concerns people's salvation, because it is the power of Christ, who heads and governs the Church, that determines the ways of her life in history.

—*Homily on the feast of St Philip, Metropolitan of Moscow*
   (January 22, 2014)

Patriarchal Ministry

176 A patriarch's cross is hard to bear, and the symbol of this toil is the patriarchal *paraman*.[10] At the same time, however, the Lord accompanies this service with great joys as well. The greatest joy for me is to celebrate the Divine Liturgy in any Russian Orthodox parish, in any monastery, or at any shrine. When I visit the remarkable holy places of our Church, I experience the divine grace that emanates from these shrines, filling the mind and heart. These signs from God are very important to me, since they come from the people: from the faithful, from priests and archpriests, and from monastics.

—*Homily on the 5th anniversary of his enthronement*
   (February 1, 2014)

[10]The *paraman* is a special square piece of cloth that the patriarch of Russia wears over his cassock, as a symbol of renunciation. At his enthronement, Patriarch Kirill said: "It is not by chance that the great *paraman* is placed on the Patriarch's shoulders as a symbol of renunciation of everything but the patriarchal ministry, a symbol of readiness to be faithful to God to the end through obedience to his will, after the likeness of the One who 'humbled himself and became obedient unto death, even death on a cross' (Phil 2.8). *Address by Patriarch Kirill of Moscow and All Russia after his enthronement at the Cathedral of Christ the Saviour* (February 1, 2009)—*Ed.*

True Joy

177 What then is joy? Joy isn't always accompanied with outward merriment. Instead of a loud laugh, it is sometimes expressed with a soft smile; and if there is laughter, it is altogether different in its quality. Joy comes from one's inner spiritual state and is a touch of divine grace, felt above all when we partake of the holy mysteries of Christ.

Joy is a quiet, peaceful condition of the soul. For those who are spiritually enlightened, it is not just a gentle state of being, but a state of heartfelt exuberance that is felt as a strong movement of the human soul. Though joy is identified with human happiness, we know that this state rarely depends on some external material factors, but is produced by a profound spiritual experience and is born out of true and sincere love.

—*Homily on Wednesday of the Fourth Week of Lent*
  (March 26, 2014)

"The word of God comes to life"

178 The word of God is the presence of God himself among us by the power of the Holy Spirit. People react to the word of God in different ways. Some arrive at correct conclusions, while others do not reach any conclusions at all; still others are bored with reading it. For the word of God to make an impact on us, we need the power of the Holy Spirit. And we know that divine energy acts and the Holy Spirit works in the Church and in the community of believers. When we stand together around God's altar and celebrate the Divine Liturgy, partaking of the body and blood of Christ, then by the power of the Holy Spirit we become participants in the Eucharist, and hence participants in all that God in Christ has done for us. Then the word of God comes to life in our consciousness and we begin to understand it correctly and to have the strength to fulfill it.

—*Homily on the feast of Pentecost at Trinity Sergius Lavra*
  (June 8, 2014)

"Patience is a fruit of God's grace"

179 Patience is the greatest Christian virtue. Ephraim the Syrian says that if we have patience, then we overcome every sorrow. This is an answer to those who ask, "What should I do in a difficult life situation? Nothing goes right in the family; work is not going right, and I don't like many things around me. It makes me annoyed and angry. How do I recover from this situation?"

What is patience, then? Is it a certain determination of the will: "I will clench my teeth and put up with it"? No, not at all! You will not go far with your teeth clenched, because eventually, they will ache! If you are unable to resist distressing circumstances, they will break you. Patience is something more than a manifestation of human will. It is always linked with one's ability to relate one's life with the will of God and to give oneself totally to God. And if we give ourselves totally to God, we will not bend before hardships, and these hardships will not demoralize us, nor will they create other conditions like depression and despair. Patience is a fruit of God's grace sent down to us in response to our humble spirits and our readiness to give ourselves to the hands of God.

—*Homily on the feast of the Icon of the Mother of God of Tolga*
  (August 21, 2014)

"The Church has something to say to modern man"

180 It is very important that the Church lead continued dialogue with our contemporaries. Dialogue presupposes exchange. The Church has something to say to modern man, but to make her word convincing, she should be able to hear what people have to say to her, understanding their sorrows and lamentations, their aspirations and hopes. The Church should not withdraw into herself. If she withdraws into her shell, she turns into a ghetto, within which people feel good because next to them are those who share their beliefs. A ghetto, however, cannot influence those around it. Precisely for this reason, the Church is called to listen to and hear people and build her pastoral programs on the basis of people's real needs.

What I am saying is not only a bishop's task; it is the task of every priest and every parish. Our parishes should be places where people flock to, not only to pray (though that is the first task) but also to find peace of soul and to be understood and supported. Each parish should become a community of the faithful bound by both beliefs and views of life, and at the same time by common good works.

—*Homily in the Trinity Cathedral in Pskov* (September 3, 2014)

The church sermon should always be relevant

181 The church sermon addressed to a community of the faithful or to those who are outside the church fold should always be relevant. It should teach one to apply the gospel to one's everyday life. Using up-to-date categories and notions, it should explain the meaning of the gospel's message to the world.

All that we do today, be it social work, youth service, or cooperation with the mass media and governmental bodies and many other things, is done by the Church only insofar as it serves the cause of human salvation. The principal mission at all times is that the Church will lead people to salvation; the Church simply does not have any other goal.

—*Homily at the presentation of the bishop's staff to Bp Flavian of Cherepovets and Belozersk* (November 23, 2014)

The New Martyrs and Confessors

182 Nothing strikes the consciousness of our contemporaries as strongly as does the tragic experience of our people, so many of whom became martyrs and confessors. It is difficult to imagine the incredible conditions in which this feat of confession was accomplished. Our persecutors would try to persuade Christians to reject their faith, threatening them with extreme penalties.

If only the answer "I believe" could have been sufficient in those days, to define one's attitude to God, to Christ, and thus seal the truth of God! But the enemy was too sophisticated, incredibly sly, and very well organized. Those who have had the opportunity to read the terrifying records of interrogation and evidence have learned that everything was handled in an entangled, crafty, and complicated manner. If we were to show the records of these interrogations to today's criminalist, he would say, "The interrogated man was an enemy"—so perfectly were the fearful accusations toward Christians created in legal terms. And yet there were those faithful who, despite the sophisticated and well-organized character of their adversary's case against them, remained capable of giving this answer to the persecutor: "I am with Christ and I do not betray him!"

—*Homily on the feast of the Synaxis of Russia's New Martyrs and Confessors* (February 9, 2014)

Martyrs are Witnesses of the Risen One

183 Martyrdom is a witness of great power. If a person dies for Christ, it means that he has a special relationship with Christ. People are not willing to die for a speculative view of some historical event or personality. It is the real faith of people that unites them with our Lord and Savior. Martyrs were those for whom Christ was alive, and they bore witness to him even to death.

Lying here at the Butovo firing range are witnesses to Christ who continued what the holy apostles did. The very fact of martyrdom in the twentieth century, almost two thousand years after the martyrdom of the apostles, testifies to their truth, the truth of God, the truth of the Church. Two thousand years after the feat of the apostles, those who bore witness to the living Christ, martyrdom was repeated in this very land. This witness to the Risen One lies at the core of our apostolic ministry and at the center of Christ's life in earthly history through the Church, which he created by his blood. Witness to the risen Christ lies at the heart of church life and church service.

—*Homily after the Liturgy at the Butovo firing range* (May 21, 2016)

"Forward to the Fathers"

184 How then do we unite tradition and modernity? Many philosophers have sought to find an answer to this question. In my view, the most successful was the answer given by Fr Georges Florovsky, an outstanding theologian and thinker of the first half of the twentieth century. Reflecting on the applicability of the patristic heritage to modernity, he came to a conclusion that it is necessary to speak of patristic synthesis. Patristic synthesis is the inclusion of the values of the heritage of the fathers in our modern culture and in modern theology. The remarkable slogan "forward to the fathers" suggests that we aren't looking backwards in a phraseological imitation of the fathers of the faith. This happens, unfortunately, in today's church homilies, when people cannot understand the language of the priest. . . .

A return to tradition is not a literary return, and not a repetition of patterns either. It is impossible to produce a copy more significant than the original. Therefore, Fr Georges Florovsky called for assimilating the experience of the holy ascetics and heading for the future!

—*Speech at the Sts Cyril and Methodius literary award ceremony*
 (May 22, 2013)

"We are not just spectators . . . during the Divine Liturgy"

185 Everything the Lord did for our salvation—his nativity and his life full of sorrows, his preaching and his suffering, the cross, the resurrection, the ascension, and his second coming—all this becomes real for each member of the Church in the mystery of the holy Eucharist. We are not just spectators of a beautiful rite during the Divine Liturgy. We, like the disciples of the Lord, are partakers of his mystical supper and his sacrifice.

—*Homily on Great and Holy Thursday* (May 2, 2013)

"What is the most important thing in life?"

186 The cross is the "guardian of the whole universe" and the triumph of the Church, the foundation for nations and countries. And it is in this understanding and experience of the power of the cross that we see the truth of divine revelation: it is not through human power, but by the power of God that we are saved.

If this is the case, if salvation is from God and not from man, then what is the most important thing in life? The most important thing is to serve God our Savior, the one who has brought this salvation for all peoples, for all epochs, and for all continents, who has opened up his embrace for all of humanity. There remains but little for us to do other than to respond to this divine action of the saving grace of God through our obedience and trust in the Lord's words and in his divine commandments.

If we assimilate the great truth that we are saved not by our own power but by God, then a great many things will be transformed in our lives. We will be able to put the priorities of our lives in the correct order and we will be able to tread the paths of our lives in peace and tranquility.

—*Homily on the feast of the Exaltation of the Holy Cross*
(September 27, 2014)

"We do not divide the Church into an earthly and heavenly one"

187 In the Church, history does not die. In the Church, the heroes we call saints are brought to life as we feel their power and presence. That is why we pray to them. That is why we build a church in honor of an archbishop who lived in the fourth century in Byzantium; indeed, we build churches and gather together in great numbers on his commemoration day, not because he is great and not because he once worked wonders, but because he works wonders today in our lives! That is why we pray to him and hear his answer.

This is how time disappears for those who are united in the Church. The Church herself is united with eternity. St Nicholas and other men of God to whom we pray are before God today, but they are also members of our Church, both the invisible Church triumphant in heaven and the Church militant in this present place and time. When we pray in church, we should understand that praying together with us are an endless number of holy ascetics, people of God, and ordinary believers—people justified by

God who are in heaven but also present with us. We do not divide the Church into an earthly and heavenly one. There is only one Church of the Lord God, which he gained by his blood.

—*Homily on the feast of St Nicholas the Wonderworker*
(December 19, 2015)

The Theotokos: Our Example

188 Today we are glorifying the most holy Theotokos, who carried her own cross throughout her life and showed us an example of holiness, purity of mind and heart, love, patience, and fortitude. She was taken up to heaven not only because she revealed in herself the greatest gift of divine grace, but also because she preserved this gift throughout her whole life. Through her patience, suffering, and sorrow, she multiplied this gift and offered a great sacrifice to God.

Today as we glorify the most pure heavenly queen, we find in her our example for how to bear our salvific crosses. We praise her as the intercessor for mankind who, having followed the sorrowful path of her earthly life, now stands in glory before her Son and our Lord and prays for us. Through her prayers, we are strengthened to bear the cross and helped along our path to salvation.

—*Homily on the Saturday of the Akathist Hymn* (March 31, 2012)

How to Feel God's Love

189 Why is it that we do not always feel God's love? Why do we sometimes neither feel God's presence in our lives nor even know what God's love is? We know what human love is. When we no longer feel another person's affection, when we ourselves are no longer in love, then no matter what declarations of love that other person makes, his or her words do not touch us. A wife may swear she loves her husband, but her words have no effect on him. A husband may cry on his knees and say to his wife, "I love you," but her heart does not respond and she "goes to a far country" (cf. Lk 15.13). Love only lives when two hearts and two human beings are joined together.

God's love has no limits—neither depth nor height, neither life nor death, neither present nor future (Rom 8.38–39). Its presence in our life depends on one thing only, our love. Without love for God we will never feel God's love, no matter how often we go to church and how many prayers we know by heart. If there is no love in our heart, God's love will not touch us.

—*Homily on the feast of the Holy Hieromartyr Hilarion (Troitsky)*
  (December 28, 2015)

The Divine Criterion of the Cross

190 St Paul says, "By [the cross of our Lord Jesus Christ] the world has been crucified to me, and I to the world" (Gal 6.14). What does "crucified by the cross" mean? Why not "on the cross," but "by the cross?" It means that the cross is the main standard and criterion of truth. It means that we should crucify on the cross our human ideas, philosophical views, and political systems, and that we should measure all these ideas by the cross in order to find out whether they are true or false. Perhaps they are just stony or thorny places upon which the word falls (cf. Mt 13.3–23). What is the rational seed in all this? The cross is a sacrifice; it is an ability to lay down your life for others. . . .

"By [the cross of our Lord Jesus Christ] the world has been crucified to me, and I to the world," the apostle says (Gal 6.14). Let us measure everything that comes to our mind by this criterion of the cross, and we will see at once the difference between truth and lies, what we should and should not vote for, what we should and should not support. This is the message of the Church! It does not interfere in the political, economic, and social processes, but holds out the divine criterion of the cross, and we are called to help people use this criterion in their lives.

—*Homily at the Patriarchal Metochion of the Holy Martyrs of Chernigov* (November 1, 2015)

The Necessity of Repentance

191 Without repentance and the awareness of one's own sins, one is incapable of opening one's heart before God. Repentance is a necessary first step toward salvation. It is not a one-time step either, because repentance should accompany a person through his or her life from youth to old age. Ideally, our every day should begin and end with repentance.

—*Homily on the feast of the Beheading of John the Baptist* (September 11, 2015)

"Faith without works is dead" (Jas 2.20)

192 The service of the good, which we call the social service of the Church, is aimed to fulfill perhaps the most important tasks. One who does them forms one's personality through good works. Indeed, there can be no Christian without good works. Faith without works is useless (cf. Jas 2.20), and at the Last Judgment the Lord will not ask us about anything but our good works: whether we gave food and drink to those who were hungry and thirsty, whether we visited those who were in hospital or prison, whether we gave clothes to the naked, and whether we sheltered a stranger (Mt 25.31–46).

It is not accidental that we will have to give account about doing or not doing such things, because without them no human personality can be fulfilled, nor can there be a human family that we describe as society. And if some believe that social work in the Church is a response to current ideas that are fashionable, they are grossly mistaken. This work is of utmost importance. If our parishes fail to become communities of healing, support, and the distribution of available resources, then we will not be able to help people find salvation.

Therefore, the Church's social work is not one of the secondary duties to be done by a rector, a parish, a dean, a ruling bishop, a patriarch, or a synod, but it is one of every Christian's primary duties. The more active this work, the more blessed our own life—ecclesial, domestic, and private.

—*Homily on the feast of the Icon of Our Lady of the Don*
  (September 1, 2015)

The Saints are our Teachers

193 The glorification of saints and celebrations in their honor give us a remarkable opportunity to think about the life of holy ones. On their special days, we can come into touch with them and through this improve ourselves, or at least begin to see our limitations in the light of their lives, and, having seen them, correct them. For this reason we call them teachers, even if they did not formally teach anybody, because their lives and their examples have great power to teach. What is left to us is to accept the lessons of their lives and their holiness, in the hope that, through their intercessions, the Lord will show his mercy to us as well.

—*Homily on the eve of the feast of the finding of the relics of*
  St Seraphim of Sarov (July 31, 2015)

The Royal Martyrs

194 Speaking about the passion-bearer (Tsar Nicholas II), we first of all remember his death, which was marked by great courage and the ability not to harden one's soul even in the face of execution. By his death the tsar showed strength of spirit, which he possessed, and which is an example for us all. That is why the tsar and his family have been glorified as passion-bearers: those who face death with dignity and who are able to meet any misfortune with dignity. Like St Job the Much-Suffering, on whose commemoration day the Tsar was born, he and his family set an example of confession of faith in the face of great suffering.

The royal family preserved the faith and their commitment to the Lord. There was no murmur against God or their persecutors. In their truly Christian attitude to sorrows, insults, and death, the last days of this family were amazing.

—*"It is important to be grateful descendants," an interview in the magazine* Foma (November 7, 2013)

"It is the cross . . . that saves you"

195 The cross is not only a one-time phenomenon associated with Golgotha and the passions of the Savior. The cross is a certain value permanently present in human life. For this reason the Lord says, "Whoever wants to follow me must deny himself" (Mk 8.34–9.1). That is, you should deny what is dear to you, what you would like to achieve, and what is really important for you. Deny these, for they are not the most important things! Take your cross, not my cross, which was the cross of Golgotha, which nobody can carry. Take your own cross and take up the suffering sent to you, and follow me.

What do these words mean? These words mean that it is the cross—the bearing of sorrows and suffering without murmur and with patience, courage, and faith in God—that saves you.

—*Homily on the Third Sunday of Lent* (March 23, 2014)

Telling the World about the Persecution of Christians

196 The Russian Orthodox Church is very much concerned over developments in the world; it is impossible to cope with some of these things on our own. Perhaps the most dreadful problem today is the persecution of Christians, and I wonder why it has not evoked a passionate response until recently. I will cite reports from international organizations: every five minutes a Christian is killed in the world, every day nearly three hundred are slain, and every year over 100,000 die. Today, Christians are persecuted in a way we have never seen, neither in the Roman Empire nor even in the Soviet Union.

And we live as if nothing has happened, since it does not happen to us, after all. In Iraq, there were a million and a half Christians. Now there are only 500,000 left. In Nigeria, radical fundamentalists commit atrocities, killing Christians and slaughtering whole villages. The same is happening in Pakistan and Afghanistan, and nobody protects them. One is killed only because he goes to church on Sunday, and nobody protects him.

I had the opportunity to visit Syria at the very beginning of the war. I saw how people live there. Horror-stricken, they fear that the hostilities will lead to the irreversible loss of their communities, as Christians will be eradicated or driven out. Later I met with the heads of many Orthodox and other Christian churches in the Middle East, and they all asked in one voice: do something, we are powerless, we are perishing! I spoke about it out loud at meetings with presidents of various countries and at international gatherings, but nobody seems to hear. . . .

Then an idea came to me, to proclaim this in a way that everyone could hear. In the course of a talk with the Pope of Rome, we agreed that we should meet and announce to the whole world the fact of the persecution of Christians. This meeting took place and the world began to speak!

—*Homily on the First Sunday of* Lent (March 20, 2016)

Pride and Humility: What is at the Center of One's Self?

197 Pride is the inner condition of the person for whom there exists only one value, that of his own ego. If at the center of one's life is one's self and everyone else takes second place, has no worth, and is marginalized, then this is pride. Outwardly, pride may even resemble humility. Sometimes people say that humility outstrips even pride. We cast our eyes down in humility and we are reticent in communicating with others, while inside we are full of pride. . . .

The humble person, though, is the one who purifies his inner expanse, drives out his ego, and concedes the central place in his life to God. Within this person's soul is a concern for others, and he perceives himself through the needs of his neighbor. Of course, in submitting to the laws of life, he needs to be concerned about himself as well and how to feed, clothe, and shelter his family, but God is at the center of his life. He cleanses the vessel of his soul, and the Lord enters into the free expanse of his human heart and bestows the special gift of grace. The more we expel our ego to the periphery of the system of values we espouse, then the more this expanse is filled by God, the greater our bond is with him, and the more abundant are the streams of grace that flow.

—*Homily on the feast of the Dormition of the Mother of God*
(August 28, 2014)

Forgiveness: The Key to Salvation

198 How are we to be saved? Today's gospel reading (Mt 18.23–35) gives the key to salvation to each of us. For those who are drawn into the merry-go-round of day-to-day life, for those of us who have darkened our minds and will, for us who have defiled our senses—we learn that the key to salvation is in our hands.

The kingdom of heaven has been likened to a king who forgave his servant a huge debt of ten thousand talents. . . . The servant came to the king, fell at his feet, and implored him to forgive him. The king forgave him. Then this man left the presence of the king, and soon came across his companion who owed him one hundred denarii, not a huge sum. The man grabbed hold of his companion by the throat, saying: give me what you owe! The companion fell to his knees and implored the man: please be patient, I have no ability to repay you just yet! But nevertheless the man forgiven by the king led his companion away to debtors' prison to be tormented until the debt was repaid.

When the king found out about this, he summoned the servant whom he had forgiven the huge debt, and gave him over to the tormentors. Since it was unlikely that this ungrateful servant would ever be able to return the money, he was beaten to death.

This remarkable parable tells us that forgiveness has a certain mystical meaning that transcends human reason. In human relationships forgiveness is a mystery. The fulfillment of this mystery bears a direct relationship to the kingdom of God: "The kingdom of heaven is like a certain king . . ." (cf. Mt 18.23). St Gregory the Theologian had these striking words to say on this topic: "Forgive, and you will be forgiven. I would suggest that this phrase be written in big letters and be hung on the wall of your room so that every day you can see them." And St Ephraim the Syrian says: "If you cannot forgive, then abandon fasting and prayer." Abandon them! They are not necessary and they are of no use to you.

How can this be? This is the very same fasting and prayer by which the demons are driven out (cf. Mt 17.21), and yet Ephraim the Syrian says: abandon fasting and prayer, they will be hollow, nothing good will come of them. You can bang your head against a wall and pray for days on end, but the kingdom of heaven will still be closed to you.

St John Chrysostom develops this topic, saying that if some-one owes you much or has offended you, hasten to forgive him, because the more you forgive, the more you will be forgiven. It comes to pass that forgiveness is a mechanism that cleanses us from sins: the more we forgive, the more we are forgiven.

—*Homily at the Divine Liturgy in the St Nicholas Peshnosha Monastery* (August 24, 2014)

The Sickness of Sin and its Cure: Love

199 The person who commits sin suffers himself and spreads his sin to those around him. Human nature is distorted, ideals are destroyed, and our feelings of responsibility, duty, truth, and love are erased, for sin does not halt but spreads. The aim of sin, the aim of evil, the aim of the devil is to ensnare all of the human soul. It begins with small acts and ends in tragedy.

We must ask ourselves: is there a means or a cure for this ter-rible sickness whose terminal metastasis spreads throughout our body and beyond us? There is a cure, and St John Chrysostom has these remarkable words to say about it: "As water by its nature washes away our bodily impurity, so too does the power of mercy cleanse our soul." The fathers in general were fond of constructing their writings around comparisons and images, and how remarkable is the image of water washing away the impurity of the human body! We feel lighter when we wipe away dirt from our bodies with water. It is in this way, and to a far greater degree, St John says, that love cleanses our soul.

We could say much on why this happens. I shall only say that sin proceeds from the fact that we expunge even God, not to mention other people, from our lives. We place ourselves at the center of our lives. This is how sin occurred in paradise at the dawn of human history. The commandment was given and God was at the center of life until Adam and Eve wanted to occupy his place, and so they fell. At the basis of any fall is the placing of oneself at the center of life.

But love, as the fathers say, obliges us to see the other person. It's not so much that we should place the other person at the center of our lives, but that we help our neighbor, and in so doing we at least in a little way make progress in giving him a place in our lives, souls, and hearts.

—*Homily on Wednesday of the First Week of Great Lent*
 (March 16, 2016)

"Our mission to be witnesses to Christ our Savior"

200 Our mission to be witnesses to Christ our Savior is one of the Church's most important tasks. It is the fulfillment of the Lord's words: "Go therefore and make disciples of all the nations, baptizing them in the name of the Father and of the Son and of the Holy Spirit: Teaching them to observe all things that I have commanded you . . ." (Mt 28.19–20). This great commission is directly linked to the main aim of the Church's existence, which is the union of people with God. Unity with the Creator is impossible without the acquisition of faith, but as the apostle Paul says, how are we to call on him in whom we have not believed? How are we to believe in him of whom we have not heard? How shall we hear without a preacher? (cf. Rom 10.14) Therefore all our church plans and energies are to be harnessed in the service of being witnesses to Christ, who is crucified and risen.

—*Speech at the opening of the Fifth All-Church Congress of Diocesan Missionaries* (November 23, 2014)

The Missionary Character of the Church

201 The Church's preaching should not be limited to the boundaries of our church buildings, and Christian community is not something contained within itself. The first preachers of the gospel were moved by Christ's call: "Go therefore and make disciples of all the nations, baptizing them in the name of the Father and of the Son and of the Holy Spirit" (Mt 28.19). He emphasizes the word "go" and reminds his hearers not to simply live within the safety of their communities. If some stranger wants to be baptized, then baptize him! This word "go" possesses all the power and meaning of the two thousand-year development of Christianity. This "go" is the essence of the missionary spirit of the Church.

—*Homily at the presentation of the bishop's staff to Bp Flavian of Cherepovets and Belozersk* (November 23, 2014)

Abundant Life and the Meaning of Love

202 Divine truth becomes manifest through the inner religious experience of the human person, and this experience helps us to understand what God in Christ, his Son, accomplished for our salvation. The Lord came and suffered so that people might have abundant life, as we have just heard in John 10.10, so that the fullness of human life will not cease with death but enter into eternity.

The Lord sacrificed all of himself and ultimately his life for this purpose. He was humiliated by human malice, envy, wrath and impurity. He was compelled by love for people—his creation—and through the example of the Lord we can understand that love, in the first instance, is the ability to surrender oneself for others. The willingness to surrender oneself and part of one's life, time, care, money, human warmth, and sympathy is a manifestation of love. Love isn't just speaking fine words, but sharing one's life with others.

—*Homily on the feast of the Great Prince St Vladimir*
   (July 28, 2009)

The Quest for Unity: "truly serving the Lord"

203 Unity is the visible image of love. If there is no unity, there is no love. And if there is no love, the loftiest Christian value, then this means that we have not assimilated the truth in full measure. That is why for Christ's followers it is so important and so necessary to preach unity.

The Savior's call for unity and the indivisible nature of his spiritual inheritance is addressed to every one of us living in the conditions of the divided Christian world. Therefore concern for the attainment of Christian unity is one of the most important obligations of every member of the Church, especially the clergy. As St Basil the Great says, "I think then that the one great end of all who are really and truly serving the Lord ought to be to bring back to union . . . [those] divided from one another."[11] It is for this reason that the holy Orthodox Church prays at each service for the "welfare of the holy churches of God and for the union of all."

[11]St Basil the Great, *Epistle 114 (110), To Cyriacus*. In *Nicene and Post-Nicene Fathers*, Second Series, Vol. 8 (Peabody, MA: Hendrickson Publishers, 1994), 190.

The way of finding unity is difficult. It is littered with a multitude of temptations, mistakes, and errors. But the fulfillment of the Savior's commandment and the integrity of his inheritance can be found on this path.

—*A Pastor's Word* (Moscow: DECR, 2008), 336

Loneliness and Finding our Neighbor

204 One of the greatest calamities of contemporary civilization is the breakdown in communication between people. Many of us suffer from loneliness. We live among people, and yet we suffer from loneliness. . . . Why? We don't live in the forest, nor in the wilderness—we have people next door to us, colleagues at work, and acquaintances all around us. So whence this acute sense of loneliness and abandonment? It is because we have no neighbors. By neighbors, I don't mean relatives that are close by or afar, or acquaintances, or colleagues and companions. No, neighbors are those who open up their hearts to us.

The Samaritan in our Lord's story became a neighbor to the man who had been attacked by robbers. This unfortunate man who had been beaten up and robbed became the Samaritan's neighbor. The mercy that we demonstrate unites people. Thus, if you do not want to be lonely, then do good deeds. Do them while you still have the strength! Even when it seems that your strength has ended and loneliness has become oppressive, still try to find those who suffer more than you do and extend your helping hand to them. In time, the loneliness will go away, for beside you there has appeared your neighbor.

Let us look a little more attentively around us: here, in our parish or in our community, someone can be found who needs our help and support. When we find one such person, if we follow the example of the Good Samaritan we will acquire for ourselves a neighbor, and this neighbor will become our brother in Christ.

There would be no wars and revolutions in the world and no terrible social conflicts and upheavals if we were able to find our neighbor. That is why the commandment to love our neighbor, along with the commandment to love God, is, according to the Savior, the greatest and most important of the commandments.

—*Homily on the 25th Sunday after Pentecost* (November 23, 2003)

"The kingdom of God is within you" (Lk 17.21).

205 The kingdom of God, which the Savior says is within every person (Lk 17.21), is the kingdom of peace, joy, truth, love, and blessedness. The kingdom of God is the fullness of life, both in this earthly life and in the life of the age to come. In the terms of our conventional human language, the kingdom of God is a great, absolute happiness that cannot be surpassed.

It is remarkable that in order to enter into this kingdom we do not need things that are deemed so essential, so desired for, and so important in twenty-first century life. In order to enter into this kingdom, we do not have to occupy an important position in society. In order to enter into this kingdom, we do not have to be powerful or enjoy authority over others. In order to enter into this kingdom, we do not need money or human success. In order to enter into this kingdom, we only have to repent—there are no other conditions. And therefore the kingdom of God is open to all, whether rich or poor, powerful or weak, or successful or not successful from the world's perspective.

—*Homily at Vespers with the Rite of Forgiveness* (March 6, 2011)

The Intellect in the Heart

206 Is it possible to attain a condition whereby zeal for the spiritual life becomes our constant companion, the permanent state of

our soul? Did the fathers and pious ascetics have a means to help them kindle within themselves this zeal, and abide genuinely and truly in a transformed spiritual state? Yes, this means does exist. The fathers describe it as the "intellect immersed in the heart" as it turns to God.

In simple terms, we are talking about permanent spiritual concentration. If in our thoughts we constantly hold within the field of our spiritual vision the state of our souls, and if we do not cease to analyze what happens in the depths of our hearts, we become capable of thoughtfully examining our words, thoughts, and actions from the spiritual perspective. The fathers call this condition of spiritual sobriety the "implantation of the intellect in the heart." In other words, in this instance the main work of our intellect is none other than the observation of our spiritual life. St Maximus the Confessor had this to say: "The intellect functions in accordance with nature when it keep the passions under control, contemplates the inner essences of created beings, and abides with God."[12]

—*Homily on Wednesday of the First Week of Lent* (March 12, 2003)

The Uncertainty of the Future and the Certainty of Good Deeds

207 The future is hidden from us, but in order to understand what the paths ahead of us may be like, we should always bear the following in mind. If we accomplish good deeds, deeds that shine; if in our actions there is no craftiness or ambiguity; and if we do not lead anyone astray in avowing certain aims while in reality pursuing others, then we can hope for God's help in these deeds. And if we want our lives to be truly peaceful, tranquil, joyful, and

---

[12]St Maximus the Confessor, *Four Hundred Texts on Love*, 4.45. In *The Philokalia: The Complete Text*, vol. 2, G.E.H. Palmer, Philip Sherrard, and Kallistos Ware, trans. (London: Faber & Faber, 1981), 105.

prosperous, we ought in our personal, family, public, and state lives to try to accomplish only good deeds. Then we will deceive neither God—though it is impossible to deceive him—nor our neighbors. And in this sense we will truly determine our fate, for if we do that which is pleasing to God, then God is with us.

—*Homily at the New Year Prayer Service* (December 31, 2015)

Vanity and Self-Examination

208 The fathers propose a means of combating vanity. We find in Maximus the Confessor unsurpassed simple words and advice, when he says that nothing so wipes away vanity as hidden virtue and frequent prayer. If upon examining our hearts we feel that particular actions have come about not because we have been motivated by good will or by striving to please the Lord and fulfill his commandments, but due to our vanity, then we ought to accomplish good deeds in secret so that not a single soul knows about them. Then everything will become clear. If we accomplish our good deeds with ease and joy, this means that we have embarked on the path of straightening ourselves out. However, if it becomes an unbearable torment to us to conceal our emotions and if there is the ardent desire to proclaim our deeds before others, then this means that vanity has enveloped our soul to such a degree that is has turned into a lethal malignant tumor.

The second word of advice from Maximus the Confessor is: pray often. This does not mean that we should recite long prayers throughout the course of the day, but it does mean that prayer as a phenomenon should be a part of our everyday lives, even if it is a momentary prayer to call upon God, to repent, to supplicate, or to praise him. And the more often we pray, the more we shall accomplish acts of charity in secret, and the less the danger of destroying all our good deeds and intentions through vanity.

—*Homily on Wednesday of the First Week of Lent* (February 25, 2015)

True Love

209 When we speak of love, we ought to understand what we mean by the word. True love is not the striving to possess another for the sake of pleasure, and it is not even feeling a sense of gratitude to another person for the good way he has treated us. Both instances are love not for another person, but for one's self. For when we love another person in order to feel pleasure in this, then the truth is that we are only showing love to ourselves through this person. When we love another only because he loves us and is kind to us, we again love only ourselves. But true love is the complete surrender of one to another. In giving ourselves and devoting ourselves to another person, we fulfill the divine commandment of the law of love.

—*A Pastor's Word* (Moscow: DECR, 2008), 91

Becoming True Witnesses of the Resurrection

210 The Christian is the one who bears within himself the light of Christ's resurrection. What does this mean? It means that the fear of death, suffering, disease, and loneliness do not determine the Christian's choices in life. The most important thing for him is only that which goes with him into eternity. In antiquity, people placed money, food, and arms in the tombs of the departed, in the belief that all of this would be of use to the deceased in the next world. But we know well that we cannot take anything from this earthly life with us into the next world, apart from our faith and our good deeds.

As the apostle and evangelist Matthew says, the Son of Man came not so that people would minister to him, but so that he could minister and give his life as a ransom for many (Mt 20.28). This example of Christ's sacrificial ministry to all people is for each one of us. . . . We become true witnesses of Christ's resurrection when we imitate his sacrificial ministry and see how the world around us is changed, transformed, and rises anew, and how people acquire new life in their desire for love and warmth.

—*Televised address for Pascha* (May 1, 2016)

The Problem of Evil and the Assurance of Faith

211 The subject of human suffering is for many a stumbling block on the path to God. And why is this so? Quite often, those on a journey toward God seek out intellectual answers to their questions. Why does the believer of great faith not ask these questions? He too is made of flesh and blood, he too is also subject to the emotions, and he too also sees suffering, including the suffering of his own children and neighbors. So why does the man of great faith not experience a crisis of faith when he encounters suffering? This is because he has the real experience of communion with God. This experience of communion with God through prayer fortifies us. We receive answers to our prayers! But it is very often impossible to explain anything to the person who does not pray and who simply says: "I cannot understand why this child is suffering, and so therefore there is no God." Yet quite often these people, while suffering themselves, encounter the divine presence and become believers.

—*Replies by His Holiness Patriarch Kirill to questions by the participants of the 5th All-Church Congress for Social Ministry* (September 5, 2015)

Love and Sacrifice

212 The apostle John teaches us that love of God and love of neighbor are inseparable (1 Jn 4.12). To allow God to occupy the central place in our lives is to give one's love not only to him but also to people. Love of neighbor and the ability to give of one's self to others are the greatest manifestations of our religious life. Why does sacrifice determine the concept of love? The answer is given by God himself, for we are told that God so loved the world that he gave his only-begotten Son up to suffering (cf. Jn 3.16). The Lord sacrificed himself and took upon himself grievous suffering and death on the cross, not because it was predetermined, but in accordance with his great love for people. St Ephraim the Syrian has these remarkable words to say: love brought down to us on earth the Son of God so that we may be saved. After the Savior's sacrifice there cannot be any doubt as to the inextricable bond between love and sacrifice: where there is love, there is sacrifice, and where there is sacrifice, there is love.

—*Homily on Thursday of the First Week of Lent* (March 10, 2011)

Bearing one's Cross

213 Even in the depths of suffering we ought always to recall that God is guiding us through life with this plan and no other, and that it is only through treading this path and fulfilling God's will that we are called to save our souls. And even if we do not have the strength to withstand at times the hard circumstances of life, we nevertheless ought to endure trials with patience, recalling that God never gives a cross that is beyond our strength. His cross does not crush and defeat us, but is given so that we may be elevated and saved. This is why there should be no despondency in the heart of the believer. But in bearing our cross that was given to us by God with humility and meekness, we ought to sustain and strengthen our faith, especially when its firmness is tested by serious external circumstances.

—*Homily on Monday of the First Week of Lent* (February 26, 2001)

"Overcome evil with good" (Rom 12.21).

214 This immortal gospel truth bears great vital wisdom: "Whoever slaps you on your right cheek, turn the other to him also" (Mt 5.39). The profound meaning of the Savior's words is revealed only to a few of our contemporaries and it is this: no evil of this world can ever pretend to obtain victory over the Christian or defile his spiritual world. Evil is never more powerful than good! As the apostle Paul reminds us, "Do not be overcome by evil, but overcome evil with good" (Rom 12.21).

To be not overcome by evil means to learn to be inured to the insults and offenses that come from people, to not take to heart another's malice, and to not allow the enemy to wound us. . . . Not to be overcome by evil means also to guard one's soul with all one's strength from the attempts to overcome it from without. It is the ability to defend the inner person from the destructive temptations of the world around us, to place ourselves on a firm foundation, and to raise a mighty spiritual stronghold for the defense of one's fragile soul. All of this requires the virtue of patience, which is why we are reminded: "By your patience possess your souls" (Lk 21.19).

—*Homily on Tuesday of the First Week of Lent* (February 27, 2001)

"A very important indicator of a person's spiritual condition"

215 The positive ability to respond with all of one's heart to the afflictions and needs of another person is a very important indicator of a person's spiritual condition. It clearly testifies to whether he is ascending the ladder to the heights of Christian virtues or, on the contrary, is crawling down into the abyss of sin. If the heart is silent, if within it there is no movement when one sees another's grief, if we do not find within ourselves either the strength or the desire to respond with compassion to another's misfortune by helping the person who needs our support, then this is a true sign of our hardness of soul, our indifference, and our inability to dispose our heart so that love reigns within it. And yet, St Tikhon of Zadonsk strengthens us in fraternal love, saying that "if you deem your neighbor unworthy of your love, then God whose servant he is and whose image he bears within himself is worthy; Christ is worthy, for he has shed his blood for him."

—*Homily on Wednesday of the First Week of Lent* (February 28, 2001)

Self-Examination: "to see one's sins and see oneself from the outside"

216 The ability to see one's sins and see oneself from the outside, and to note our bad actions, mistakes, and transgressions against the Lord's commandments, are all signs of a healthy spiritual life. Truly, there is no man who lives and sins not. Through our own weaknesses and through the power of the passions and temptations that beset us, we can retreat and fall into sin. In contemplating our sins, examining them close up and condemning them and sincerely confessing our guilt before God, we should in no way hasten to forget what we have done as soon as possible. Instead, we should repent with contrition in confession, so that we may cleanse our souls and approach the chalice of the Lord without condemnation.

Indeed, the Savior came into this world to call not the righteous but sinners to repentance, as the gospel says (Mt 9.13; Mk 2.17). And in the days of his earthly life the Lord forgave repentant sinners, and before his ascension to the heavenly Father he gave to the apostles and those who came after them the power to forgive people's sins in his name. "What sins should be forgiven we should not even need to inquire, for the New Testament makes no distinction and promises remission of all sins to those who repent worthily," is how St Basil the Great explains the Lord's forgiveness of all.

—*Homily on Friday of the First Week of Lent* (March 2, 2001)

The Sacraments: Christ's Life in our Lives

217 Christ forever and again renews our lives in the sacraments of the Church. The mystery of the Eucharist revives within our souls and memories all the acts that Jesus accomplished and all the events linked to him, and by grace we become witnesses to them and participants in them. In the mystery of baptism we relive the saving Passover of the Lord with Christ, dying together with him and rising with him to new life. In the mystery of chrismation, each of us personally relives Pentecost, the descent of the Holy Spirit upon the apostles, for we partake in the reception of the gift of the Holy Spirit. Thus, in the Church's sacraments, by the power of the Holy Spirit, we become real communicants and co-participants of all that God in Christ has done for our salvation. And the fruit of this for us is communion with God and his bestowal upon us of the gift of the grace of divine energy, with which the Lord blesses us and sustains us.

—*Homily on Saturday of the First Week of Lent* (March 3, 2001)

"What does it mean to turn toward God?"

218 At the foundation of all movement toward God lies our turning toward him. . . . But what does it mean to turn toward God? First of all, it means we recognize the fact that God *is*, that he exists, and that his presence in our lives is extremely important. But to recognize with our intellect the reality of God's existence is insufficient. Complete turning toward God happens when we are not only convinced of the existence of God, but are ready to dispassionately examine the recesses of our hearts and respond honestly to the question of what really is the true condition of our souls. . . .

Turning toward God means simply the ability to be aware of our sins and to see our own falsehood. In the words of the remarkable prayer of St Ephraim the Syrian, we ask: "O Lord and King, grant me to see my own transgressions. . . ." In other words, we ask God to grant us the ability to see our sins, for without an understanding of what is happening in our hearts, we shall never be able to cleanse ourselves of sin—and only the pure in heart shall see God (Mt 5.8). Turning toward God opens up the ability for us to see our own sins and falsehood. With this begins our spiritual ascent—the beginning of all good transformations.

—*Homily at Vespers with the Rite of Forgiveness* (March 17, 2002)

"Christian mercy always reflects God's mercy"

219 When viewing a person's deeds, Christian mercy always reflects God's mercy. The Lord is compassionate toward people, not only when they suffer innocently, but also when their afflictions are a result of their own errors and when they have brought misfortune upon themselves. And it is not only on those who are kin in flesh and spirit that we ought to spread our Christian mercy, but also upon every human being as God's creature. God's goodness is magnanimous and compassionate, and his mercy makes no distinction among people. Ultimately, his compassion is active and practical, bearing genuine fruit.

—*Homily on Tuesday of the First Week of Lent* (March 11, 2003)

"The things that are in heaven . . . united to the things that are on earth"

220 In striving for heaven and eternal salvation, the Christian should never accomplish his journey toward salvation by offending his kin and those close to him by renouncing good family relationships, or by in any way insulting someone's dignity. Sin is not within human nature, but rather exists in perverted human will. Those labors that we do for the glory of God are blessed by God. . . . Human creativity, both the lofty and the insignificant, is our gift to God, a sacrifice that we offer to God. If we understand human life, human nature, and human relationships in this way, then our relationships will be filled with divine grace. Then, as the apostle says, the things that are in heaven will be united with the things that are on earth, and God will be at the head of all things (cf. Eph 1.10), filling and sustaining all things through his power.

—*Homily on the feast of the Synaxis of the Most Holy Mother of God* (January 8, 2010)

Each person is unique "because this is what God desired!"

221 It pleased the Lord that each person should be unique. There are no two people who are the same, and each has dignity before the face of the Lord regardless of social position: whether they are famous or not, educated or uneducated, occupying an important occupation or simple one, rich or poor. Each person has his or her unique traits, because this is what God desired! And we must recognize this divine plan for the human person and remember that we should never envy anyone, for everyone has their own life, works within their own capabilities, and journeys along their own unique path. If the Lord gives a gift to someone that provokes envy within us, then we ought to remember that either God has thereby bestowed his blessing upon this person, or has allowed it.

—*Homily on Tuesday of the First Week of Lent* (March 19, 2013)

Respect, not Envy

222 The awareness that each person is a child of God with his peculiarities and distinctions helps us to experience a sense of respect toward other people. When we respect others, we are close to the path of feeling love for them in our hearts. Envy always blocks our love for one another, and it is the most terrible obstacle toward realizing God's main divine commandment to love God and our neighbor (cf. Mt 22.35–40).

—*Homily on Tuesday of the First Week of Lent* (March 19, 2013)

The Path to Forgiveness and Grace

223 What is required of us so that we may merit the forgiveness of the Lord and acquire his grace? A little is needed: first, strong belief that only God saves us on our journey through life and beyond. Nobody and nothing other than this: neither leaders, nor patrons, nor our own strength, nor our gifts and talents, nor money, rank, position, or social standing, but only and exclusively the Lord God is the sole giver of earthly good things and our true Savior in eternity. "Put not your trust in princes, nor in the sons of men, in whom there is no salvation" (Ps 145.3). . . .

Second, to acquire God's grace, we have to be aware of our own sin. If we lose this ability, then morally and spiritually we die and we are unable to seek out the path leading to paradise lost, wherein we enter into communion with the Lord. In this instance we have chosen to slam the door shut behind ourselves that leads into the kingdom of God. By contrast, if we give an account of our bad acts and see our own sins, then we retain the ability to repent, and this means we can receive forgiveness from God.

—*Homily on Forgiveness Sunday* (February 22, 2004)

The Experience of Grace and Everyday Life

224 Each of us to one degree or another has encountered what we may characterize as the presence of God's grace. This occurs during worship, especially during the celebration of the mystery of the Eucharist, and through the mystery of the baptism of adults. It happens when we are alone at prayer, especially if we are monks. . . . And for people who live in the world, this is sometimes linked to those wonderful feelings we experience when we contemplate the beauty of nature, or the handmade beauty of the works of great artists who have faith in their hearts and who have created masterpieces of representational art. Sometimes we experience God's grace when we hear especially inspired works of music that touch our souls. Through all of this we meet God, for God is behind all genuine creativity, and we experience a certain inner transformation.

This feeling is especially powerful in those who have abandoned non-belief for faith and who, having encountered God, genuinely feel his presence and believe that they will now begin a new life since all that is old is now in the past. . . . But then it transpires that something else is happening within our lives. We come down from Mt Tabor and once more find ourselves in the thick of the crowd, in the midst of everyday life with its temptations, problems, and conflicts; how often we lose this inspiration. . . .

And here we cannot but recall the words of the apostle Peter, who went through all of the things we have been through, yet even more dramatically. He lived through the renunciation of the Savior and in a wondrous manner expressed his spiritual experience of being on Mt Tabor and the subsequent renunciation:

"Therefore, brethren, be even more diligent to make your call and election sure, for if you do these things you will never stumble" (2 Pet 1.10).

—*Homily on the feast of the Transfiguration of the Lord*
(August 19, 2013)

"*Repentance is the most important thing in a Christian's life*"

225 Repentance is the most important thing in a Christian's life. It presupposes an inner in-depth self-analysis, a critical appraisal of one's thoughts and actions, and a constant struggle with one's weaknesses. This requires constant and unceasing self-perfecting. It is also what distinguishes a human being from animals, which simply are not capable of moral self-perfection, and which at best carry out commands and are accustomed to submitting to the human person. Moral self-perfection is a characteristic of man alone, for he possesses an immortal soul destined for life everlasting. And in order to attain this eternity, we have to elevate our souls here in this earthly life by working on ourselves every day. This work is called repentance. It contains the power, meaning, and perhaps even the drama of human existence, yet the human person has no other path.

Since this truth is revealed to us in the word of God and in the Church's teaching, then we are to receive it, remember it, and try to live in accordance with it. We become a person primarily as a result of this inner struggle with ourselves and of our efforts at self-perfecting. There is no other goal higher than this. Everything else is secondary, formal, and bears no relation to the main goal of the Christian, which is life everlasting in God.

—*Homily on Wednesday of the First Week of Lent*
(February 25, 2004)

The Church's Mission: "only in carrying our cross and speaking in love"

226 Today I address our priests and I call upon them all to be bold, strong in faith, courageous, and at the same time good shepherds. The good shepherd lays down his life for his sheep. . . . We must not . . . participate in public polemics in a way that does not befit a Christian; with humility and simplicity of heart we should bear our witness to both society and the whole world.

Some may think that this is already a no-win situation—that this is the position of the weak. Yet acting with humility and simplicity is what we do when we follow Christ, for he saved the human race not through the power of authority and human might, but through the cross and love. . . . And it is only in carrying our cross and speaking in love that the mission of the Church in the contemporary world is capable of transforming people for the better and opening up the gates of the kingdom of heaven to many.

—*Homily on the feast of St Philip, Metropolitan of Moscow*
   (July 16, 2011)

"We are drawn to Christ still, because he is the Son of God"

227 Our salvation comes through the Son of God's entrance into the world, who ascended the cross and endured disgrace and affliction for the human race. This truly does lie outside the bounds of human logic. How then is it that people today still ponder the meaning of what the Savior has accomplished? Why are we so attracted to his image? Why have people looked upon him and reflected on their own lives for two thousand years, in spite of the fact that his system of values and his commandments are observed with such difficulty? We are drawn to Christ still, because he is the Son of God. All that our Lord has done has been

accomplished because he is God himself. " 'For my thoughts are not your thoughts, nor are your ways my ways,' says the Lord" (Is 55.8).

—*Homily on the feast of the Exaltation of the Holy Cross* (September 27, 2010)

Love: "A New Commandment" (Jn 13.34)

228 Shortly before his sufferings on the cross, in his farewell conversation with the disciples Christ said: "A new commandment I give to you, that you love one another" (Jn 13.34). What is new in all of this? It is that God henceforth brings forth his supreme judgment not according to the laws of formal piety, but according to how we relate to our neighbors and what we bring them—joy, peace, and goodness; or, on the contrary, trouble, hatred, and enmity.

In addition, we know that our God, who became man and rose from the dead, is not only the judge, but also the Savior. He is the way and the truth and the life (Jn 14.6). Christ not only brings forth judgment; rather, he also becomes the advocate of every sinner who turns to him in faith. The most important spiritual requirement of the New Testament is that we love one another in spite of all our differences. A deficit of love destroys the human person, divides families, and destroys society and the state.

—*Televised address on Pascha* (April 20, 2014)

Gratitude, Humility, and Confession

229 The feeling of gratitude ought to accompany each of us, beginning with our gratitude to God. ... St John Chrysostom had these remarkable words to say: "Although our gratitude cannot add anything to God, it does bring us closer to him." Why does thanksgiving to God bring us closer to him? Because when we thank God (or even a person, for that matter), consciously or unconsciously, we push our ego aside. Whether we are aware of it or not, we admit the role of God or of another person in our lives, because God or our neighbor who has been good to us has done that which we could not do. In giving thanks we confess our limitations, our lack of absolute power, and our inability to do everything for ourselves.

At the same time, St John Chrysostom remarkably says: "Thanksgiving to God is none other than the confessing of our sins." We may think, where is that connection? Yet the connection is a direct one. If we give thanks to the Lord, then we understand that what he has done we could not have done ourselves. And this self-critical, wise, sober attitude toward ourselves cannot but turn our minds toward our own weaknesses and our sins. Therefore, thanksgiving to God within ourselves contains our readiness to bring repentance too. That is why thanksgiving is a great act in our religious life. We beseech God, we give thanks to him, and we glorify him in our prayers. Inasmuch as we give thanks to him, we draw close to him.

—*Homily at the Cathedral of the Holy Trinity and St Vladimir in Novosibirsk* (August 24, 2013)

Hope: "we can see all . . . refracted through the prism of faith"

230 "Put not your trust in princes, nor in the sons of men," the word of God teaches us (Ps 145.3). Place your hope in God. But hope in God should not free us from the awareness of our responsibility for our lives and actions, for if this were the case, then our personal mistakes and even crimes could be blamed on hope. The person who lives with faith in God, filled with hope in the Creator, possesses an inner strength to solve all the tasks set

before him. Unlike the one who has no faith or hope in God, this person is never subject to a sense of despondency. Like the non-believer, he may endure harsh circumstances, but he will never feel despondent, for what despondency can there be if God is alongside him? And even if God allows us to be lonely, ill, or in difficult circumstances, we can see all of this refracted through the prism of our faith. Above us we see the hand of God, and thereby we can acquire a peaceful, tranquil, and assured view of our lives.

—*Homily on Monday of the First Week of Lent* (March 7, 2011)

Mercy: "Good deeds should not be something out of the ordinary"

231 Mercy should be an integral component of a Christian's life, not occasionally but constantly. We are to define for ourselves an area where we can do good, and each is to have his own "zone of responsibility": we care for our parents, especially when they become old and infirm; we care for children, especially when they need it; we care for our friends and relatives, who might be in difficult circumstances or suffer from illnesses; and, finally, we care for those whom we know to be going through difficult times. . . . The accomplishment of good deeds for those in need should not be for us something out of the ordinary; rather, it should be an organic and permanent part of our lives. A life without charity, good deeds, and compassion should be impossible for us.

—*Homily on Tuesday of the First Week of Lent* (March 15, 2005)

The Mystery of the Church, Beyond the Barriers of Time

232 All that the Lord has accomplished for our salvation—his birth, his life and teaching, his miracles and suffering, death and resurrection, ascension and sitting at the right hand of the Father, and his glorious and awesome second coming (as we say in the prayer at the Divine Liturgy)[13]—the Holy Spirit mystically makes all of this our inheritance by removing the barriers of time. There is no time with God, and by his grace he makes us participants of all that Christ accomplished and continues to accomplish.

This co-participation in the life, sufferings, death and resurrection of the Savior is a mystery incomprehensible to the human mind, a mystery of the Church. All of history is contained in the Church of God: by the power of the Holy Spirit, the past, present, and future become the inheritance of those who comprise the Church: the living, the departed, and those yet to be born.

—*Homily on Friday of the First Week of Lent* (March 10, 2006)

"The hope by which we live"

233 We believe that God will save us, and this will happen not because we are strong, powerful, and able to achieve our own salvation, but because through the suffering, death, and resurrection of the Lord, the Holy Spirit gives us the possibility of becoming co-participants of his saving mission and his redemptive sacrifice. Thanks to this incomprehensible, sacred, and mighty deed accomplished by God in his love for the human race, we have the hope by which we live. We strive toward God in our prayers and thoughts, recalling our sins and repenting of them, but without despairing and falling into despondency. Despair and despon-

---

[13]In the liturgy, after "Drink of it, all of you . . ." the priest says, "Remembering this saving commandment and all those things which have come to pass for us: the cross, the tomb, the resurrection on the third day, the ascension into heaven, the sitting at the right hand, and the second and glorious coming," and the prayer continues with the exclamation: "Thine own of thine own, we offer unto thee, on behalf of all and for all." This points to the eternal and eschatological character of the liturgy: only by "removing the barriers of time" can we *remember* the second coming.—*Ed.*

dency are sinful, for we are all called to life in God and with God. And God in Christ, by the power of the Holy Spirit, grants to us the necessary strength and steadfastness to work out our salvation with humility and hope in his will.

—*Homily on Friday of the First Week of Lent* (March 10, 2006)

"Liberation from sin is both a human and divine action"

234 Repentance is an act accomplished by us with contrite hearts aware of the wretchedness of our lives and the sinfulness of our existence. At the same time, repentance is a divine act. In response to our prayer and our repentance, and through the visible absolution of our sins by the priest, God grants to us forgiveness and remission of our sins. We simply cannot forgive ourselves of our own accord, for here no spiritual endeavors, fasting, asceticism, or prayer vigils can help; God alone can forgive our sins. His divine act is interwoven into our penitential endeavors, and this is why liberation from sin is both a human and divine action.

—*Homily on Monday of the First Week of Lent* (February 19, 2007)

Building up the Church, Glorifying God

235 The apostles did everything they could to strengthen their faith in the Lord and Savior, so that they in turn could strengthen God's Church. Even to a little degree, our labors should be aimed at an affirmation of the faith, so that the life of the Church might become ever more bright and effective. Then we shall have the boldness to ask of the Lord: "Help me, for I am concerned not only for earthly things and not only for myself, but I desire that your name be glorified in my children and grandchildren." It is my deep conviction that this will be so with every person who in the name of God and without protest overcomes difficulties, and who devotes even a small part of his life to the glory of God.

—*Homily on the feast of the Holy Apostles Peter and Paul*
  (July 12, 2016)

Afflictions Reveal God's Presence in our Life

236 The holy monastic fathers not only did not run away from suffering, but they immersed themselves in a special situation where nobody could help them to overcome difficult circumstances. They abandoned the world, renounced the support of society, and rejected money and power. . . . Why was this necessary? It was necessary so that not in words, not from books, but from their own experience of life, they could understand that the greatest power that exists is the power of God.

When we encounter dangers in our lives and when we endure afflictions with God's aid and with great faith surrender ourselves to the divine will, then the only salvation for us is God. And of course this way of life brings people into special contact with God. God ceases to be simply a word, an abstract concept, or a nebulous idea. He is next to us at every moment of our lives, and an unbreakable bond is established between the human person and God. People acquire a completely special way of life, in which the border between earth and heaven and between the divine and the human is erased.

—*Homily for the feast of Sts Zosima, Sabbatius, and Herman of*
  Solovki (August 21, 2009)

"The kingdom of God begins here on earth"

237 We should let God reign over us. It is not God who by his might and boundless power subjects us to his will, but we who subject our wills to God. When the Lord said the well-known words: "The kingdom of God is within you," (Lk 17.21) he . . . showed that the kingdom of God begins here on earth. It is impossible to live in hell here and to inherit the kingdom of God there. It is impossible to do works here contrary to the will of God—to multiply sin, falsehood, lies, and to work not for God but for the devil—and then to find ourselves in the kingdom of God.

We should place ourselves under God's power while we are here on earth. . . . This placement will be a result of our free will. And we should simply seek to fulfill as far as possible the commandments of God; they are so simple and clear! It is through fulfilling these simple and clear commandments that we will let God rule over us, and then the rays of this eternal kingdom will reach us although we live in the midst of human deception, malice, and sin. Indeed, if God rules over us, then we too will live in his kingdom, and even if this kingdom is not around us, then according to the word of God it will be within us.

—*Homily on the feast of the finding of the head of St John the Baptist* (March 12, 2011)

How to Bear Our Crosses

238 Passion is the domination of the desires of the flesh over the human spirit. Why does one's addiction need to be overcome in order to assume one's cross? The relationship between the domination of a passion and the corresponding inability to overcome real suffering is asserted so vividly and clearly by the word of God. A person who lives under the power of a passion is unable to bear the cross. He is weak; he has neither patience nor courage and he is not free, because the passion rules over him. Only a spiritually free and strong person can carry his cross properly. That is why it is impossible to assume the cross without rejecting oneself. Without rejecting the passions, no bearing of the cross will emerge. . . .

On the other hand, a person who overcomes a passion sets his soul free from the last of his flesh and will find power and patience and inner freedom. And then any assumption of the cross, any overcoming of suffering that life sends us and the Lord gives us, becomes a good and light burden.

—*Homily on the Third Sunday of Lent* (March 27, 2011)

Prayer for the Dead

239 We remember the dead in prayer, first of all, in order that their sins may be forgiven and that they may be acquitted before the judgment seat of God. The Church is given this strength and power to pray and change the afterlife fate of her members, her faithful. The Lord has given this power to us who live on earth not according to our merits or because we are so close to him, but only because the Son of God suffered and arose from the dead. In this action, he acquitted the human guilt of the fall and took upon himself the guilt for the sins of all people, delivering us from sin. When one of us dies while bearing a sin, then by the power of the Holy Spirit this sin can be forgiven through the prayers of the Church.

—*Homily on Tuesday of the second week after Pascha*
  (May 3, 2011)

How the Church Must Speak to Young People

240 When I speak of the need for us to learn the language intelligible to our youth, I do not mean slang, jargon, or the fashionable, popular ideas of the youth milieu of the moment. I mean that when the priest or a preacher addresses a young audience, he needs to get into the heart of the real, vital, and spiritual problems of the new generation, and to give cogent answers to them on the basis of the word of God. We have no other ground for dialogue with the world, but we should formulate God's word to the youth in simple and clear language. We must be sincere, relate to the real needs of the young person, and be imbued with love for these people regardless of how friendly or open they are to us.

If young people feel that the Church addresses them with sincere love, that our fraternal benevolence is inspired by a warm and open feeling, and that our attitude is marked by friendly readiness to reach out rather than the desire to impose our system of values on them, then these young people will listen to us.

—*"To be a religious person in one's youth is the mark of a spiritual gift," a speech at the Orthodox Youth Congress* (May 15, 2001)

"In service to others . . . man finds real happiness"

241 God has so ordered human nature so that it is precisely in service to others that man finds real happiness. The more lofty and full-blooded the service he renders, the fuller the happiness. The service of Christ, which begins with simple good works and an attempt to live in accordance with his commandments, brings happiness to man. This joy begins on earth but continues in eternity, making man a participant in eternal life.

—*Address on Orthodox Youth Day* (February 15, 2009)

"The condition for accepting salvation"

242 The Lord came to deliver us from the power of our own sin, and he accomplished this mission of salvation. However, we know that all that the Lord accomplished does not extend to us magically and automatically. The greatest mistake made by many

Christians is that they believe that God has saved us and that no more effort is required from us.

Yet St Paul, saying that the Lord came to save sinners from their own sins, points out the most important thing: "I am the worst of the sinners" (cf. 1 Tim 1.15). He reminds us that the condition for accepting salvation is that we be aware that we are more sinful than others. So, if we can carry out inward examination in order to become aware of our vital failures and our personal sin, only then will the Lord's free gift be extended to us too.

—*Homily on the 35th Sunday after Pentecost* (February 3, 2013)

The Question of God Cannot Wait

243 The question of whether there is a God or no God, and to believe or not to believe, is not a question we should wait to answer. We can't afford to think, "Now I will settle all the things of this world, and then when I retire, I will ponder spiritual things and go to church." No, our disposition, our vital philosophy, and ultimately our happiness will flow out of how we decide this issue. The Lord said, "I am the way and the truth and the life" (Jn. 14.6), and I believe each of these words. I believe that he is the way and the truth and the life, and, since this is so, I should follow his way in order to have the truth and full life.

—*Speech at a meeting with youth and students in Moscow*
  (May 23, 2009)

The Church's Witness: "a balance between the eternal and the changeable"

244 The Church preserves the Scriptures and the tradition intact; the eternal and unchangeable God gave them to us. At the same time, however, we do not conceal the word of God from people;

we do not go away to catacombs. Therefore, in fulfilling our duty of preaching entrusted to us by our Savior, we should endeavor to be understood correctly and speak to people so that they can understand us. The task itself—to bring the good news about the crucified and risen Christ—presupposes that it should be actualized. For this reason, in the Church's witness before the world, it is necessary to observe a balance between the eternal and the changeable. If this balance is broken, then the preaching either slides down to servility to human passion or, on the contrary, becomes so "elevated" as to become unapproachable and pharisaical. Those who preach Christ need talent, sensitivity, the ability to condescend to human weaknesses, and sincere love of people, above which is only the love of God.

—*The Patriarch and the Youth: Talks without Diplomacy*
    (Moscow: St Daniel Monastery, 2009), 139–140

Spiritual Growth: Learning, Experiencing, Acting

245 A believer should continually develop his mind and educate his mind for faith, doing it not only, as the apostle said, to give an answer to those who ask (cf. 1 Pet 3.1), but to become stronger in the faith. This strengthening of faith helps to make his mind more agile, but also through faith his whole human being is enveloped in godly power.

When faith begins to live in one's heart, one comes to feel the presence of God. Now God is revealed to man not in logical constructions or intellectual proofs, but in the real experience of life. When a believer feels the presence of God in prayer, or when he senses God during the partaking of the holy mysteries of Christ, for instance, the believer knows for certain that this presence is from God and it is God's gift in his life. He can say for sure: this happened to me by God's mercy and by God's will; it is God's presence in my life. And then faith becomes so strong that the will is strengthened as well, and one is able to live in accordance with the faith, to do good works, and to share one's experience with others.

—*Homily on Bright Monday* (April 21, 2009)

The Word of God: "the immutable criterion"

246 What can help people in any circumstances, despite any lures and temptations, to preserve the great and saving ability to distinguish between good and evil? Scripture says, "The word that I have spoken will judge him in the last day" (Jn 12.48). It is the word of God that contains the immutable criterion of the difference between good and evil, the indisputable truth. Even if everybody around you begins saying something contrary to the word of God, you should understand that all the arguments of the majority are actually based on errors and deception.

When a believer aligns his life with the word of God, he safeguards his inner freedom against external circumstances and thus avoids becoming a puppet in the hands of others; he escapes the manipulation of those with evil will and intentions. The word of God gives the believer an opportunity to remain free and to preserve his ability to distinguish between good and evil.

—*Homily on Great and Holy Tuesday* (April 18, 2006)

"How do we take in suffering and sorrow?"

247 How do we take in suffering and sorrow, which are given in human life and cannot be excluded from this life? . . . When the Lord visits us, bringing sorrow and often suffering, we should not become fainthearted or lose faith. Moreover, we should never murmur against God. We should take in suffering as something given and at such moments never compare ourselves to others, saying: this one seems to be worse than me, but he does not suffer.

Indeed, we do not know what is going on the lives and souls of other people. Our task is to meet our own sorrow in dignity and not to let it destroy the integrity of our personality, weaken us, or make us unhappy. And we should carry our cross with commitment to the will of God, remembering that to bear the cross with dignity is a necessary condition for true superiority. By superiority, we do not mean a vain superiority that is formed by human customs, political power, or wealth, but true superiority before God that alone has eternal value.

—*Homily on the Fifth Sunday of Lent* (April 6, 2014)

"Glorify God in your body and your spirit" (1 Cor 6.20)

248 The Apostle Paul calls us to glorify the Lord in our souls and in our bodies, which are God's (cf. 1 Cor 6.20). Today's feast of the Synaxis of the Theotokos emphasizes the relationships of the Savior with His family and those around Him, and thus calls us once again to live a pious life, to have good relationships with our neighbors and our relatives, and to build human relationships in accordance with God's commandments. In this way, we may truly glorify God both in our souls and in our bodies.

—*Homily on the feast of the Synaxis of the Most Holy Mother of God* (January 8, 2010)

"Good is a great power"

249 St Paul says astonishing words: "If your enemy is hungry, feed him; if he is thirsty, give him a drink. For in so doing, you will heap coals of fire on his head." He concludes this thought with remarkable words: "Do not be overcome by evil, but overcome evil with good" (cf. Rom 12.20–21).

Anyone who does not believe in the gospel and does not understand the Savior's words about how one who is slapped on one cheek should turn the other cheek should reflect on these great words, "overcome evil with good." Good is a great power. If evil is overcome with evil, then the one who is stronger physically will win, whereas if evil is overcome with good, then the one who is stronger spiritually wins. . . .

There is something even more essential for understanding how good saves us. . . . What happens when we respond to evil with evil? We lose our inner peace, and the foe has defeated us. Why does evil coming from another person change my inner world? Why does the other defeat me and cause me to lose my peace? It happens each time we respond to evil with evil. In this way, we are already defeated, and evil prevails in our heart. There was peace; now there is no peace. There was quiet; now there is no quiet. . . . Do not let evil conquer you!

—*Homily on the feast of St Sergius of Radonezh* (July 18, 2016)

What Helps Us Bear Our Sorrows?

250 There is no one born who will enjoy happiness and well-being all the time from birth to death. Everyone has his own sorrows. Someone has family troubles, for someone else nothing goes right at work, another has lost his job, and someone else is lacking money for a life of dignity and to support his family. In searching for some human ways of settling these earthly, everyday problems, we should always rely on our faith in order to keep our spirit quiet, to preserve our vital guidelines, to avoid substituting our values, and to keep from losing God's truth. It is the truth that helps us live and bear our sorrows.

—Homily in the Cathedral of the Resurrection at Narva (June 15, 2013)

Our Responsibility for the Gifts of God

251 We should be aware of our great responsibility before God for the gift we have received at baptism, for the grace we receive in the sacrament of the Eucharist, and the power we receive in prayer. These are the gifts of God, and we are possessors of these gifts. To make sure that the power of grace never leaves us and that we do not turn into empty vessels, we should keep seeking the grace of the Holy Spirit through prayer, good works, participation in the sacraments of the Church, and the proclamation of this grace to the whole human race; in other words, good works and good words.

—Homily on the feast of Pentecost (June 23, 2013)

"When I am weak, then I am strong" (2 Cor 12.10)

252 Love always works with a special force where mental and volitional resources are exhausted and there is no inner strength to fulfill what you should fulfill. Love makes up for all our weaknesses because it is the totality of all perfections. If you have love in your heart, this great feeling that we address to God and our neighbors offsets all our weaknesses and our shortcomings, for it is accepted by the Lord as a fragrant and most precious gift.

—Homily on the eve of the Transfiguration of the Lord
   (August 18, 2013)

The Suffering God and the Mystery of Life and Death

253 The cross is in the center of our whole life. And who is on the cross, but a crucified man? . . . Why did the Lord wish it to be so?

He willed it thus in order to save people through his cross, and because he wished to get down to the very depth of human suffering. Nobody can murmur against God and say, "Why should I endure this suffering at all?" If God had appeared before us in glory as a Roman emperor on a chariot, all in gold and silver, then everyone could have said, "Why do you abandon us and allow us to suffer?" But he himself went up to the cross and suffered as no other did. For this reason there can be no murmur against God in the human soul.

The mystery of life and death is in his hands. No human being comes to the world apart from his will, and no human being leaves this world without his will. We do not know why different people find themselves in different circumstances—some die earlier, while others die in old age. This is concealed from us. Therefore, we should accept everything that happens to us, both joys and the deepest sorrows, as that which is present in God's design.

—*Remarks at a meeting with widows and mothers of miners who
died in the Kuzbass region* (August 25, 2013)

"The true quality of a human"

254 There is not a single person who has lived through his whole life with ease. Everyone has invisible flaws in his heart, and everyone can say that he or she has experienced difficult moments in life as deep tribulations. But we little think of the fact that, though these tribulations are caused by external circumstances, the experience itself belongs to our inner spiritual nature. This experience is within us, while a person standing next to us may not feel the same, since it is we who suffer or rejoice for some reason. This ultimately means that happiness or misfortune is caused by one's perception of the surrounding world. . . .

Those who are far from the Church sometimes ask us, "And how can you help?" . . . We give this answer: through the Church and through the community of the faithful who assemble in church for prayer, God himself touches our souls. We depend on him throughout all that befalls our souls—be it happiness or misfortune, joy, peace, and quiet, or shattering sorrow and disappointment. The totality of all these feelings determines the true quality of a human life, and to make this quality of life high, one should always remember to depend on God for the health of one's soul. Then, both in marshes and in mires, in hard work or in ease, one will be able to preserve inner peace and quiet, finding happiness.

—*Homily at a Prayer Service in the Dormition Cathedral in the Pühtitsa Patriarchal Convent* (September 20, 2013)

"*Have peace in your heart, and millions around you will be saved*" *(St Seraphim)*

255 In some sense, each of us is really an architect of our own fortune, not only in the sense that our external wellbeing depends on our choices, but also in the sense that each of us forms our own inner world. If this formation takes place with God's participation, this world becomes a reflection of the divine world. There is the remarkable example of St Seraphim of Sarov, who said, "Have peace in your heart, and millions around you will be saved." A person who bears a reflection of the divine paradise in his heart becomes a radiant and attractive personality capable of influencing the lives of others.

—*Homily at a Prayer Service in the Dormition Cathedral in the Pühtitsa Patriarchal Convent* (September 20, 2013)

"And who is my neighbor?" (Lk 10.29)

256 Doing good works transforms strangers who are not familiar with each other into neighbors. It is difficult to sacrifice something for the sake of a stranger, but it is easier to do it for the sake of one's neighbor. A neighbor becomes known not from his family tree, not from his identity papers, but from the experience of life. When we do good to each other, we become neighbors, and one can do very much for one's neighbor. . . . How remarkable are the words of St John Chrysostom: "How can you hope that God will give you what you ask if you did not give to your neighbor?"

. . . And when we call out to God insistently, saying, "Help me," let us recall whether we ourselves helped anybody. If we did not, we should stop praying this, because our prayer will not reach God's throne. Instead, we ought to go and do something good for those whom we once rejected, or for one whom we encounter on our life's path. If in addressing the Lord we can then say, "Lord, help me, for I too as a weak man help other people as much as I can, living according to your commandments," then the Lord will hear our prayers.

—*Homily at the Divine Liturgy in the church of the Descent of the Holy Spirit in the village of Pervomayskoye* (November 24, 2013)

The Unknown Future and the Lord of History

257 An unknown future is ahead of us. Scientists seek to forecast developments, while futurologists describe a remote future, but nobody actually knows what will come to pass. Only the Lord is the Lord of history and the historical process, in which all that we participate in is in his hands. We know for sure that where God is, life is. We know for sure that where there is no God, is death. For this reason, to have a hope for the future, we should rely in the first place on divine law—above all human laws—and subject human laws to this moral divine law and live according to it, transforming our minds and our hearts. Then we will have a clear, peaceful, and favorable prospect for life. Where God dwells, there is peace, patience, mercy, and the manifestation of the best human feelings.

—*Homily before a New Year Prayer Service* (December 31, 2013)

Divine Grace and Human Efforts

258 Interaction between divine grace and human efforts can be compared to the movement of a sailing vessel. The vessel can be excellently equipped. It can have a remarkable professional crew. Yet if the wind does not blow into the sails, the yacht will not move, and if there are no sails, the wind will blow in vain. The wind is like the action of divine grace, while the sail is like a human being with his earthly affairs. How we build and order our life will determine whether the divine wind will fill the sails of our life or not. To make this happen, it is necessary that those who steer the boat should understand how to set the sail.

This is precisely the mode of interaction between God and human beings, both in our personal life and in the life of society, the state, and the entire human race. If we seek to build excellent super-technological vessels but do not ask for the power of divine grace to fill the sails above us, then our efforts are in vain.

—*Homily on the feast of Sts Sergius and Herman of Valaam* (July 11, 2016)

The Apostolic Cry: "May our Lord come!"

259 Let us walk through life continuing the ministry of the pre-eminent apostles as much as we can, aware that anyone baptized in the name of the Father and the Son and the Holy Spirit is called to the apostolic ministry. That is why we also call the Church apostolic: not only because in the beginning of her history there were apostles, but also because she is fulfilling the great apostolic mission.

Through centuries, through cultures and civilizations, through peaceful times and terrible upheavals, the Church is rushing to meet God the Savior as he comes to us from heaven. The great exclamation of the first Christians, "Maranatha!" or "May our Lord come!" (1 Cor 16.22) is the exclamation of the whole apostolic Church. The whole assembly of the faithful who over many generations have preserved their faith in the resurrected Lord and Savior will come out to meet the coming Savior halfway.

—*Homily on the feast of Sts Peter and Paul* (July 12, 2016)

The Broad Path and the Narrow Path

260 The miracle of the existence of the Church in history for two thousand years, accompanied with persecutions, schisms, divisions, the miracle of the fact that the Church exists today and we can assemble for prayer, for the celebration of the sacrament of the Eucharist and for partaking of the body and blood of the Lord—all this shows that God himself through his Spirit is present in the community that is called the Church, which was founded by the apostles. The apostles laid the foundation. They could not and must not have tried to foresee all the subsequent cultural and intellectual development of humanity. And even if they could foresee all that, they could never have created a community of importance for each subsequent time, and even less for each nation and each culture. It was impossible to do it and it was not the task that the Lord called them to do. He called them to go and become witnesses to him who was raised from the dead, to go even to the end of the world to teach nations what he taught them (cf. Mt 28.19–20). And this was the foundation on which the apostles themselves began to erect the building of the one, holy, catholic and apostolic Church. It is impossible to say that the building was unfinished at that time. It is finished at each moment of time. At each moment of time the fullness of the Holy Spirit is in the Church; at each moment of time, the fullness of truth that cannot be overcome by any human false wisdom and even by "the gates of hades" (Mt 16.18) is in it.

We believe that the gates of hades will never shake the Church. We believe that the foundation built by the holy apostles will endure even the most terrible earthquakes. However, while believing this, we should also accept our responsibility for enabling the Church living today to preserve her spiritual power and the ability to address herself to the nations with apostolic preaching. It requires the talents of all people, of the young and old alike, to safeguard her, to take an active part in her life, so that through inner work, including intellectual work, we may free church life from possible shortcomings and imperfections, becoming a community of ardent faith, a community of like-minded people who continue the ministry of the holy apostles in history. We believe that through their intercession the Lord will bless the apostolic ministry of our Church.

—*Homily on the feast of the Synaxis of the Twelve Apostles*
(July 13, 2011)

Self-Mastery or the Slavery of Sin

261 A man loses freedom when he ceases to master himself, when he stops controlling his thoughts and actions, when he becomes a slave to his passions and sin, and when he becomes weak and incapable of withstanding the pressure of external circumstances. It often happens not because the circumstances are so hard, but because we ourselves are not free inwardly. When you read the lives of the saints, you are struck by how much the venerable ascetics were free. Nothing could make them gloomy and nothing could upset their routine, because they had conquered their own selves. When we attain inner freedom and victory over our own selves, it opens up for us the possibility of being truly free.

—*Homily on the feast of the Annunciation* (April 7, 2016)

The Power of God's Love

262 God's love is a great power! We become aware of this only when we ourselves love God. The love of God begins with small things indeed, with a prayer that we try to pronounce not mechanically but from the heart, thoughtfully. The love of God begins with a small sacrifice offered to those in need, when we share our good fortunes with others or do other good works for them. It is in the depth of these actions that the seeds of the love of God grow ripe.

That is why to live a Christian life we need not only to attend church, not only to observe fasts, and not even only to be priests. Both the priest and the layperson can live as Christians only when the love of God truly emerges in their hearts. And if this love is there, it becomes a great power that cannot be overcome by height or depth or life or death or the present or the future (Rom 8.38–39).

—*Homily on the feast of the holy Hieromartyr Hilarion (Troitsky)* (December 28, 2015)

"A great mystery of human happiness"

263 The Lord tells us that all who are weary and burdened (Mt 11.27–30), tired, sick, disillusioned, both believers and non-believers, should come to him, and he will give them rest. Why? He is humble and meek of heart. . . .

If humility and meekness give people rest, and rest is almost a synonym of happiness, then what great power humility and meekness possess! And when we are disturbed by all that happens in the world as we desire to carve out a career, earn more money, obtain more power, and achieve new social heights, we realize that there is no rest in life. It is only a continued struggle in which permanent demanding challenges wear us out. . . .

The Lord reveals to us a great mystery of human happiness; we only need to abide with him, remembering that the greatest power that transforms the human heart and gives consolation, peace, and quiet in any sorrow is humility and meekness. This is not weakness. We know how humble and meek people are capable of giving their lives for their neighbors and for the motherland. Humility and meekness are not synonyms of weakness. They are synonyms of happiness.

—*Homily on the eve of the Synaxis of the Optina Elders*
  (October 23, 2015)

Decision-Making in the Church

264 We believe that the Church of Christ is one holy, catholic, and apostolic, as it is clearly stated in the Nicene Creed. The Church is one in her nature. The presence of many autocephalous churches in the world is a form of the Church's life in history, the most suitable for carrying out her mission of salvation.

We also know that the decision-making in the Church, significant for all the Orthodox plenitude, has always required the participation of, if not all the Orthodox hierarchs, then at least representatives of each local church. In this sense, Ecumenical Councils and some other councils of pan-Orthodox significance are a visible expression of the unity of the Church and her conciliar nature, a reflection of her self-awareness as one body in Christ (cf. Rom 12.5). At the same time, the reception of the actions of a particular council has always been gradual and, as the history of the Church shows, no council could impose its decision if they proved to be rejected by the people of God, if there was no reception of a council's decision by the whole Church. Therefore, no Ecumenical Council became such merely by the fact of its convocation: its real significance became evident only after some time, sometimes a very long time.

—*Speech at the Bishops' Council of the Russian Orthodox Church* (February 2, 2016)

What is a Great and Holy Council?

265 A Great and Holy Council, if correctly prepared, can become an important factor of consolidation of inter-church unity and cooperation and help clarify the answers the Orthodox Church gives to the questions of the present on the basis of her age-old tradition. It will be pan-Orthodox only if representatives of all the generally recognized autocephalous Orthodox Churches are in attendance.

—*Speech at the Bishops' Council of the Russian Orthodox Church* (February 2, 2016)

"The meeting in Crete can become an important step"

266 Brothers, we all are the one Body of Christ (cf. 1 Cor 12.27). We have received the priceless gift of unity from the Lord and our Savior Jesus Christ himself. To preserve this gift is one of our principal tasks; it is a direct commandment of our Savior (Jn 17.21).

Let us not be confused by the fact that the opinions of sister churches about the convocation of the Holy and Great Council have been divided. According to St Paul, there must be factions among you in order that those who are genuine among you may be recognized (1 Cor 11.19). In the days of preparation for the Council, such differences have become fully revealed, but we must not allow them to weaken the unity that God commands, to grow into an inter-church conflict, to bring division and trouble into our ranks. We remain one Orthodox family and together we all bear responsibility for the fate of Holy Orthodoxy. . . .

I trust that if there is a good will, the meeting in Crete can become an important step toward overcoming the present differences. It can make its own contribution to the preparation of that Holy and Great Council which will unite all the local autocephalous churches without exception and become a visible reflection of the unity of the holy Orthodox Church of Christ, for which our predecessors, who passed away in peace, prayed and which they expected.

—*Message to the Primates and representatives of Local Orthodox Churches assembled in Crete* (June 17, 2016)

The Plight of Christians in the Middle East

267 In the twentieth century, the Russian Orthodox Church experienced terrible persecution for the name of Christ and cannot stay indifferent to the persecution, suffering, and killing of people for their belonging to the Christian faith. According to St Paul, "If one part suffers, every part suffers with it" (1 Cor 12.26). This became the principal incentive for my meeting with Pope Francis of Rome on February 12, 2016 in Cuba. In the Joint Statement signed as a result of the meeting, there is a call to the world community to do all that is possible to stop violence in the Middle East, which is impossible to do without coordinated actions of all the forces opposing extremism. I am convinced that by uniting the efforts of East and West, in bearing witness to the forces that actually seek to eliminate Christianity in the Middle East and some other regions, we will be able to fulfill our calling in the world more effectively.

—*Speech for the 70th anniversary of the Department for External Church Relations of the Moscow Patriarchate* (May 19, 2016)

"The Church's sphere of influence is the whole human race"

268 It is with attention and responsibility that I take the criticism against inter-confessional contacts expressed by some of the clergy, monastics, and laity, not only of the Russian Orthodox Church, but also other local Orthodox Churches. I have always believed and continue to believe that their voice should be heard and understood. It is necessary to conduct an open and honest dialogue with those who really aspire to the truth and are sincerely concerned about the purity of Orthodoxy and the good of the Church. . . .

Constructive and benevolent criticism should be distinguished from the accusations sometimes leveled against the Church by those who are infected with a sectarian outlook; they call the Church to withdraw into full isolation. The sectarian outlook is one that suggests that, for various reasons, the Church should separate from the world and from its principal mission to bring light to people. It is expressed, among other things, in the demands that the Church should limit her relations with the world around her in accordance with the tastes and interests of those who make such proposals to the Church. However, the Church cannot let herself be led by such recommendations, even less by any such demands! The Church's sphere of influence is the whole human race, the whole world, and people of all ethnic backgrounds, views, and political beliefs.

—*Speech for the 70th anniversary of the DECR of the MP* (May 19, 2016)

"The gospel and tradition are about the future and for the future"

269 As we celebrate, we confess the same faith and lift up essentially the same prayers as many of our ancestors did. Tradition, however, is not only a way of meeting the preceding generations. We address tradition not because we love antiquity, but because what is conveyed in it is the saving truth. Indeed, as St Paul says: "Jesus Christ is the same yesterday and today and forever" (Heb 13.7). Our future and our hope are in our holy Orthodox faith. Let us not forget that the gospel is given to us for the transfiguration of man, so that we may know what kind of man one can become if he follows Christ. In other words, the gospel and tradition are about the future and for the future, not only and even not so much about the past.

—*Speech at the Bishops' Council of the Russian Orthodox Church* (February 2, 2016)

Transforming Ourselves Can Transform the World

270 We all want to change the world around us and make it better, purer, kinder, and fairer. In the gospel, we find an utterly clear indication of which path should be followed by those who care about changing the world and our present reality. This path is Christ! The Lord says, "I am the light of the world. Whoever follows me will never walk in darkness, but will have the light of life" (Jn 8.12). What does this mean? It means that we should make efforts to follow Christ and build our life in accordance with the gospel's ideals. As we transform ourselves and our inner world and mature spiritually, we will be able to transform the world around us by the power of God's grace.

—*"An Apostle of Russian Unity," an address to the 23rd International Christmas Educational Readings under the name "Prince Vladimir: The Civilizational Choice of Rus'"* (January 21, 2015)

The Church's Mission: "to bring people to Christ and to save human souls"

271 In all times, the principal and invariable goal of the Church's mission is to bring people to Christ and to save human souls. According to the wise providence of God, we do not achieve salvation on our own, but together in the community of the faithful. The Lord himself, who created the Church on earth and gave to all her members an unalterable promise that "the gates of hades will not overcome it" (Mt 16.18), has ordained this.

Reflecting on this divine determination, the holy fathers unanimously testify that outside the Church, this community of the faithful, there is no salvation. Now a parish is a part of the greater church family, a lesser community of the faithful in which people who gather around the eucharistic cup find real spiritual unity through mystical unity in Christ. That is why the development of community life and the active involvement of the faithful in it is a task that is of vital and critical importance for the Church.

—*Report to the Bishops' Conference* (February 2, 2015)

"We are called by the Lord 'to preach the word'" (2 Tim 4.2)

272 It is important to talk to those who don't have clergy mentors and spiritual authorities. Yes, it is sometimes difficult. But notwithstanding all the difficulties, we are called by the Lord "to preach the word . . . convince, rebuke, exhort, with all longsuffering and teaching. . . . But you be watchful in all things, endure afflictions, do the work of an evangelist, fulfill your ministry" (2 Tim 4.2, 5). With benevolent persistence filled with apostolic zeal, without any feeling of superiority, we should go to general education schools, libraries, and cultural institutions with words about God, whose presence is creatively, albeit sometimes unconsciously,

reflected in the life of the whole creation through authentic cultural creative works. We should go to social institutions in which, through our deeds of charity and words of compassion, we can bear witness to the good news of the gospel. Any formalism is unacceptable here, as when a priest reads a speech at a charitable institution, then listlessly distributes gifts prepared for the needy, and quickly departs. "Be of one mind, having compassion for one another . . ." (1 Pet 3.8). Each priest going to preach, especially in an external environment, should firmly remember these words of the apostle.

—*Report to the Bishops' Conference* (February 2, 2015)

"For everyone to whom much is given, from him much will be required" (Lk 12.48)

273 As His Eminence Nikodim (Rotov) used to say, one must do everything possible to make the most of the opportunity of serving and ministry in the Church. One could let things slide in one's service, treating one's parishioners formally, coming to and leaving the church, and collecting one's pay. . . . His Eminence Nikodim did not serve in this way. Wherever he was, he put his whole self in the task and used to the full the existing opportunities for the sake of fostering church life. These opportunities were humble and small, which makes the feat of such people as the late Metropolitan Nikodim remarkable. The opportunities in our time are tremendous, and to extract all possible things from these opportunities is much more difficult today than it was at that time. What is needed is sound and ardent faith, boldness before God, and solid knowledge; modern man has more confidence in those who know more. What is required is love for people and the willingness for sacrificial service. God grant that all this is present in today's clergy. Remember this precept of the late Metropolitan Nikodim—extract everything possible from the opportunities open to the Church. Perhaps this is the only way of salvation for us as servants of God, for much is expected where much is given.

—*Homily at the church of the Holy Prince Dimitry-on-the-Field in Uglich* (September 9, 2010)

We Must Account for How We Use Our Freedom

274 It pleased God to put the gift of freedom into his creation. In finding our divine program for life, we can either develop the gifts that God has given us, or destroy and ruin them—it is our free will and choice. The Lord gave to one person a good memory and a sharp intellect, but he ruined both his memory and intellect by heavy drinking, and became an invalid in his prime. He lost everything and it was his choice. He will give an account for this choice before God.

Or, on the contrary, one received a gift from the Lord and toiled all this life, mobilizing his resources, big and small—here everything depends on God. Great talents, whether one has ten talents or one or half a talent, are given by the Lord. It is for us to develop and offer them as a fragrant sacrifice to the Lord. We offer our lives, our work, our feats, whether big or small. This is the domain of our freedom—to drink or not to drink, to sin or not to sin, to believe in God or not to believe, to build churches or to destroy them. We are free in all that. But we will be called to account for this domain of freedom at the great Last Judgment. The Lord will not ask us, "Why did you not have talents?" But he will ask, "Why you did not use your five talents to produce ten? Why did you bury your talent in the ground? Why did you not live as I taught you to live?"

—*Homily at the Divine Liturgy at the Cathedral of the Dormition in Yaroslavl* (September 12, 2010)

Church preaching calls
"all people to a life not of this world"

275 Preaching in our churches is aimed not so much at settling momentary problems faced by people, though good advice based on the gospel can be very useful for that. But the principal task of the Church is to bring all people to a life not of this world, but life in the kingdom of God. This life begins here on earth when we feel the presence of grace in our hearts, and then it continues when we meet Christ after our death.

The Church has a transcendent, trans-temporal mission, and it is for this reason that people plunged in the everyday bustle of daily life so often misunderstand the meaning of church preaching. It seems obsolete to some and unintelligible to others, because the Church speaks not of the vanity of the earthly world, but invites everybody to come in touch with the heavenly world.

This heavenly contact is not only concerned with the afterlife and one's preparation for the heavenly kingdom. This connection has much to do with our earthly life because when we feel God's presence in our hearts, we come to have a reference point and a coordinate system. We come to know exactly what should and should not be done in all the circumstances of life, and the Lord himself tells us that his yoke is easy and his burden is light (cf. Mt 11.30).

If we are in the Church and have this encounter with God's grace, experiencing it as the good and perfect yoke of God, then our human life becomes easy and blessed. Even in the vortex of our everyday chores and in the bustle, we suddenly begin to become aware of the eternal and immutable things of life and feel as if our wings have grown.

—*Homily on the feast of the Protection of the Theotokos*
   (October 14, 2011)

Self-Knowledge and Self-Control

276 Self-knowledge and self-control are indispensable conditions for the growth of the human personality. It is easy to draw an analogy here with our ordinary life. If one does not wish to know the surrounding world, if he does not wish to learn anything, then he can hardly achieve anything in his life. Moreover, if he does not control his actions and words, then how many if not sinful but simply erroneous things can he do, which will disturb his life? And if all that is true for our everyday life and our relations with the world around us, then it is all the more true and necessary for our inner life.

—*Homily on Tuesday of the First Week of Lent* (February 24, 2015)

Dialogue: Bearing Witness to Christ

277 We are called today to serve the world and to bear witness to Christ before those who are near and who are far. This calling requires us to enter into dialogue between the Church and the state, between the Church and society, between the Church and the world of science and education. We are also called to serve the world through interreligious dialogue. Through our dialogue in all these spheres, the Church brings to people—not by power or arms or coercion, but by the power of the word of God—those ideas without which it is impossible to build a truly human private and public life.

—*Homily on the feast of St Philaret, Metropolitan of Moscow* (December 2, 2014)

External Hardship and Inner Spiritual Struggle

278 It is not accidental at all that the venerable fathers headed for places in which life was especially difficult, because external hardship and the need to overcome it steel the human soul, while comfortable conditions deaden one's strength, weaken one's mind and will, and make one incapable of both spiritual and vital feats.

This striking link between spiritual feats and difficult external circumstances should make each of us ask ourselves: what am I doing and in what conditions do I live? Can my living conditions and my inner disposition help me perform feats, including the most important and difficult ones that involve the education of my inner self? Do my circumstances aid me in overcoming my own sins and weaknesses and my own dangerous inclinations, so that I may reach a higher state of soul and spirit?

Of course, not each of us is capable of saving his soul in difficult external circumstances. We should be grateful to God for our ordinary life, then, although we so often complain that it is too difficult. But if the Lord gives us difficult external circumstances, then we should accept these circumstances with gratitude to God, treating them as especially favorable for our spiritual fight and the struggle for our own salvation.

—*Homily on the eve of the Transfiguration of the Lord*
  (August 18, 2014)

The Humility of the God-Man and the Queen of Heaven

279 When we look at the image of the Savior, especially that of him sitting on the throne, we see him as the Pantocrator. It is difficult for us to see all the humility and simplicity of the God-Man, a simple carpenter who walked the dusty roads of Judea and Galilee, sharing food with fishermen, publicans, and sinners. He was not squeamish about anything. He did not shun anybody. He was there amidst human suffering, and his most holy mother was there together with him. . . .

When we bow before the image of the Mother of God during the feast, we see the heavenly queen in glory. It is difficult for us to see how simple she was and how belittled, yet this is the authentic image of the most holy one! And even today, standing in glory before her Son, she stands before him in humility. That is why she hears the prayers of all those who are hungry and thirsty, who are suffering, who are sick, or who simply need help. She hears this prayer and lifts it up to the throne of her Son.

This is why the heavenly queen is so greatly venerated. This is why there are so many images painted in her memory. This is why such a great number of feasts are devoted to her, since she, being the queen of heaven and earth as the mother of the Son of God, has given us an example of a life that should also become our life. She has revealed to us the power of humbleness and meekness. Still, today, she helps us to assimilate the divine system of values, as it is only by adopting this that one can have fullness of life and have it abundantly.

—*Homily on the feast of the Smolensk Hodegetria Icon of the Mother of God* (August 10, 2010)

The Apostolic Ministry of an Archpastor

280 I have often heard this question: Is there a certain ideal image of the archpastor, or some obligatory set of personal characteristics necessary for a bishop? . . . The moral requirements to be met by future archpastors are very high and strict. But this is not the sum of human traits that each hierarch should have, since the image of a worthy bishop is not just a collection of virtues necessary for his ministry. What sets a real archpastor apart is this very important ability: he can make the gospel's message relevant and valuable for people today. Just as the apostles brought to the world the joyful news about the Savior who arose from the grave, so a bishop should humbly, courageously, and convincingly bear witness before those who are near and far to our risen Lord Jesus Christ. In this way he continues the great apostolic ministry to be a witness to the risen one, even to the ends of the earth.

—*Homily at the presentation of the bishop's staff to Bp Ignaty of Armavir and Labinsk* (April 13, 2014)

How to Know and Understand Ourselves

281 If we do not seek to know ourselves and if we do not understand ourselves, then even God is helpless to save us. This isn't because he has no power, but because he has granted man freedom and he does not force anybody to seek salvation. . . . And how then can one know oneself? Basil the Great says that it is impossible to see oneself by ordinary sight; even our mind hesitates when it examines its own shortcomings, yet becomes acute when examining the weaknesses of others. Our mind is insightful and strong when we look closely into the faults of other people, but lingers and hesitates, according to the saint, when it is necessary to look into our own sins.

Therefore, the human mind is a means of knowledge of oneself, yes, but not only the mind. St Nicetas Stithatos tells us what one should do to sort out one's own inner spiritual life and understand one's faults. Indeed, he reminds us of two very important conditions: first, we must practice detachment from our everyday cares, and second, we must continually practice the testing of one's own conscience.

—*Homily on Monday of the First Week of Lent* (March 3, 2014)

"Contend earnestly for the faith which was once for all delivered to the saints" (Jude 3)

282 The Church's march in history is through the way of the cross, predicted by her divine Founder and Head, our Lord Jesus

Christ. We cannot say that we have gone through all our trials without consequences and loss, for there were and are manifestations of human weakness in the Church, shortcomings in interchurch communion and differences and misunderstandings on some issues. For the last two millennia, however, we have managed by God's mercy to preserve the most important thing, the purity of the saving Orthodox faith and our unity. We should guard this treasure as the apple of one's eye. Only in this case we will be able to bear our witness successfully and be the light of the world and the salt of the earth (cf. Mt 5.13–14), standing as the pillar of Christendom.

—*Speech at the grand reception in honor of the participants in the Meeting of Primates and Representatives of Local Orthodox Churches* (March 9, 2014)

Service in the Church: "there are no useless gifts"

283 Service is not an obligation or a duty: it does not have to be "worked off" but, rather, it is performed. The ability to perform well and sincerely one's service in the Church, whatever it may be—from that of a patriarch's service to that of an ordinary candle woman's task—is a gift of God. It is an opportunity to attain "to the measure of the stature of the fullness of Christ" (Eph 4.13). In the Church, one is given the gift of a particular service to the extent of his aspiration and achievement, as well as to the extent of human resources and ecclesial necessity. In God's wisdom and goodness, he has ordained it so that there are no useless gifts; the usefulness of these gifts lies in the building up of the one body of Christ, as each member discovers his true nature and fulfills his calling through living participation in this body.

—*Homily at the Divine Liturgy in Christ the Savior Cathedral* (January 26, 2014)

The Church: "all the people of God united around her bishop"

284 It is wrong to suggest that the Church is only the hierarchy—bishops, priests, deacons, or those who work in the Church. The Church is made up of all the people of God. She reveals herself when she celebrates the divine Eucharist around her bishop or priest, and everyone in the Church has his particular service.

Laymen and women, as baptized members of the Church, are not "extras." A layperson is one who carries out a special service in the Church. To be lay is also a service, and we are dedicated to this service through the sacrament of Baptism. Therefore, when it is only the hierarchy or clergy who do everything in the Church and the laity is only present at the liturgy, than it is very dangerous for the life of the Church. This attitude fails to acknowledge the most important principle of church life: the Church is a community of faith and includes all the people of God united around her bishop.

—*"A Pastor's Word," the patriarch's TV program* (May 28, 2011)

"The Church needs young people today"

285 It is very important that the faithful realize that the service of the Church is the common task of all her members, from the layperson to the patriarch. Indeed, it is the involvement of all the people of God in church work that creates authentic community and life in the Church. Membership in the Church should never be understood as the mastering of certain external skills; rather, it should be seen as the living relationship of the believer to his community, as he shares in the life of his parish and the whole Church.

This is especially true for the youth. It is not always easy for the older generation to find a common language with young people. Sometimes we even hear this opinion: let them grow up, it is said, and face problems, and then they will come to the Church on their own. But this is wrong! The Church needs young people today. We should boldly involve them in the Church's work, thus transforming the youth from being objects of our care into living missionary workers and witnesses to our Orthodox faith by their words and lives.

—*Interview with the press service of the Ukrainian Orthodox Church* (July 15, 2009)

"The way to the Council"

286 The way to the Council is a way of growth in love and unity. . . . It is not a desire to win, to assert one's views, but respect for the opinion of the other, the readiness to take into account as much as possible the position of each Church that lead us to the desired unanimity, thus speeding up the pre-Council process. Our interactions should be centered on the commandment that the Lord has given us to love one another (Jn 13.34). We feel this love during the Divine Liturgy. . . . Being sometimes proponents of different views, we sincerely say to one another, "Christ is in our midst" and sincerely respond, "He is and shall be."

—*Speech at the grand reception in honor of the participants of the Meeting of Primates and Representatives of Local Orthodox Churches* (March 9, 2014)

A "Christ-Culture"

287 There are two tasks faced by Christians: they should have a good knowledge of modern man—his wishes, aspirations, and interests—and should seek to transform this culture on Christian principles to make it a "Christ-culture," to use the term of Nicholas Berdyaev and the venerable martyr Maria Skobtsova.

. . . The Church's tradition teaches that it is possible and important to assert Christianity both through the ascetical experience
of rejection of the world, and through the use of secular philosophical categories and scientific and cultural achievements. The
holy fathers sought to bring the Church to the external world by
accepting all beneficial things while rejecting sinful things. To do
this, they were in continual dialogue with the state and society,
even when both society and the state were not Christian.

—*"The Russian Church and European Culture," in the journal*
Ekspert, *Issue 4/690* (2010)

Freedom from *Something or Freedom* for *Something*

288 Christianity offers the most convincing worldview for modern man. Indeed, if freedom is the ultimate value for the person
of our time, then it is in the person of the God-Man Jesus Christ
that human nature has attained the ultimate freedom from evil
and sin. Christianity offers a vision of freedom much loftier than
simply the negative notion of freedom *from* something—freedom
from exploitation, violence, and restriction. In Christ Jesus a person can attain the freedom *for* something—freedom for his full
self-fulfillment in the love of God and neighbor. It is in the har-
monious synergy between God and man, as Christianity teaches
and as was achieved in the lives of the saints and ascetics of the
Church, that each can find an answer to the tormenting problems
of freedom and the meaning of life and social service.

—*"The Russian Church and European Culture"* (2010)

A New Language for Preaching Christian Values

289 Christians have to find new languages and new creative ways
of preaching Christian values in today's continuously changing world, to enable this preaching to be heard and properly

understood. The sphere of culture is the area in which constructive dialogue between the Church and society can be the most effective, and I see here an opportunity for fruitful cooperation between Christians who uphold traditional values. In the first place, I mean the cooperation between the Roman Catholic Church and the Orthodox Church, which have a common social and economic view of the pressing problems of social and economic ethics, bioethics, the family, and personal morality. Our common Christian tradition, commitment to dialogue, and readiness for cooperation can and must become a driving mechanism of mutual rapprochement.

—*"The Russian Church and European Culture"* (2010)

"You are the temple of God" (1 Cor 3.16): "the lofty calling of man"

290 "Don't you know," the apostle says, "that you are the temple of God and that the Spirit of God dwells in you? If anyone defiles the temple of God, God will destroy him" (1 Cor 3.16–17). These words point to the lofty calling of man and the human body. According to the apostle, our bodies are God's vessels and temples. Just as we revere handmade and restored churches, so each should revere his body, designed by God as the temple of the indwelling Holy Spirit.

And what does it mean to destroy God's temple? It means to destroy human nature. It means to direct a human life along the way that does not correspond to God's design. It means to oppose God and become an enemy of God, and the enemy of God is the devil. The devil infuses us with various thoughts, influencing our consciousness, our will, and our feelings in order to pervert all until our bodies are destroyed. Therefore, the greatest struggle waged by man is the struggle with one's self, as one endeavors to remain God's temple and to preserve the presence of the Spirit of God.

—*Homily on the feast of the Translation of the Relics of Sts Zosimas and Sabbatius of Solovki* (August 21, 2016)

"*I am the way, the truth, and the life*" (Jn 14.6)

291 The question of true faith concerns many people, both those who have merely come into contact with religion and those who already live by the laws of faith. Do we Christians have reason to insist that our faith is true and saving? Yes, and it is contained in the farewell discourse of the Savior with his disciples, when Christ said: "I am the way, the truth, and the life. No one comes to the Father except through me" (Jn 14.6).

These words contain an answer to the question on true faith. If Christ is the way, the truth, and the life, if no one can come to the Father other than through the Son, then it follows that he is the true way for us to God. And this is why the answer of the believing Christian to the question of other religions ought to consist of the following: we do not know and cannot say whether other religions bring people to God or not, for this is hidden from us and God alone will pass judgment on this. But we know precisely that the Lord Jesus Christ is the way, the truth, and the life, and that he grants to people the possibility of entering into communion with the heavenly Father.

—*A Pastor's Word* (Moscow: DECR, 2008), 327

The Gift of Grace

292 "But grace was given to each one of us according to the measure of Christ's gift" (Eph 4.7). What does this mean? This means that each person has received the gift of grace by God's will. . . . God participates in the life of people by the gift of grace, and it depends on him to give the gifts according to his measure. This gift does not depend on one's background, on whether one was born to a noble or ordinary family, or on what education one has. This gift depends even less on one's property or social status or success in one's work. The gift of God's grace is divine inspiration, which gives one the strength to fulfill the will of God.

"And he himself gave some to be apostles, some prophets, some evangelists, and some pastors and teachers, for the equipping of the saints for the work of ministry, for the edifying of the body of Christ" (Eph 4.11–12). Not everyone is given the gift of the episcopate but only those whom God elects. Not everyone is given the gift of priesthood, but only those whom God elects. Not everyone is given the gift of prophecy, teaching, and ministry, but only those whom God elects. It cannot be said that one gift is more pleasing to God than the other. It cannot be said that one gift is higher or more significant in God's eyes than the other. Each of us has his own gift and his own ministry, significant in the eyes of God. This is the basis of the conciliar ministry of the whole Church, in which the episcopate, clergy, and laity carry out multiple ministries in the Church, and they stand together before God in prayer.

—*Homily on the Sunday after Theophany* (January 23, 2011)

"The most important thing in our spiritual life"

293 We should understand what the most important thing in our spiritual life is. It seems to us that it is important to reach a certain height and a certain status, be it an external position in society, in the family, or in a high office or a rank. Many associate success with intellectual development and a good education. Many believe that with these benefits comes culture, and then this successful person will hold to a certain level of ethics. What is important to God, however, is not the static condition of a person who is satisfied with his inner life; what is necessary to God is that one has a dynamic development toward perfection.

—*Homily on the Sunday of the Publican and the Pharisee*
(January 24, 2010)

Today's Struggles

294 We venerate the holy martyrs for revealing the great and saving power of God through their torment and suffering. The example of the martyrs helps us understand what the power of God means, as applied to human life and the human personality. We see in their example how God elevates man, how he makes him strong and invincible, and how he gives man the ability to resist evil and persecution, even up to terrible pain. Martyrs stand before us as real heroes of the spirit, and we humbly bow before them, praying to them as living examples of that which God does with those who open their minds and hearts to God. . . .

At the same time, to become a confessor of the faith of Christ and to be faithful to the Savior, it is not necessary to prove it by physical suffering. Certainly, the martyrs faced a great temptation when their persecutors suggested that they reject Christ and thus be allowed to lead a quiet life and go back to their homes. But there are temptations we face today too; we must choose either to remain with Christ, undergo trials, and walk the narrow path, or choose to reject him and take the universal broad path of those who focus on the enjoyment of temporal pleasure and the pursuit of material gain. . . .

What is required of a Christian today is courage, patience, a strong will, and, most importantly, we need trust in the Lord. We receive him in our hearts in order to stand firm in the temptations of life. . . . And what is required of us today, too, is faith in Christ and faithfulness to the Lord. Today's struggles are not any less than they were in the old days, only now the temptations and lures are more sophisticated.

—*Homily on the feast of the Holy Martyr Tryphon*
  (February 14, 2009)

The Fruit of the Spirit: Peace, Joy, and Love

295 The fruit of the Spirit is love, joy, peace, forbearance, kindness, goodness, and faithfulness (Gal 5.22). What values can be higher? Peace means tranquility, good relations with those around us, and absence of danger. It means we don't have to fear someone burning our homes, looting or robbing us, or attacking us from without or betraying us from within. Peace is the fruit of the Spirit we value most in our relationships.

Then we speak of joy. What a great mistake our contemporaries make when they confuse joy with laughter and merriment. Laughter passes so quickly that nothing is left of it; indeed, sometimes only a very bad aftertaste lingers on. Joy is not laughter, though it may be accompanied with laughter and a smile. Joy is a special state of the soul in which one needs nothing more. One is satisfied and this satisfaction is reflected in one's inner life in the awareness of a sense of well-being.

And, finally, we honor the spiritual fruit of love. People are capable of doing all kinds of things to win love: they pay money to earn it and commit betrayals and crimes when it is withheld, but still love does not come. People marry and then realize within a few years that there was no love present at all, and that their marriage was a mistake built on an illusion. Real love, on the other hand, is a glorious and divine feeling, which, together with joy, gives us this fullness of life in the Spirit. Love is a state of the heart that reaches up to God and out to one's closest relatives and friends, those with whom one has contact, and then radiates even to those who are far off and to the whole creation itself, both inanimate nature and the animal kingdom. . . .

What can be compared with such values as peace, joy and love? St Paul teaches us that these values are not from us. We might exert every effort yet still not obtain peace. We can pay enormous sums of money but never have love. We can laugh at the top of our voices until we cry yet still not experience real joy. Peace, joy, and love are gifts of the Holy Spirit.

How important it is that people should learn and understand this! Without the Holy Spirit there are no gifts of the Spirit, only a dreadful race. Like a hamster running in a wheel, we, in a rush to obtain what we seek, nevertheless do not acquire these gifts. The Church is called today to use her loving voice, one full of compassion for people's suffering and for life's tragedies, to tell people that the greatest values for us come from God, not from us. It is the gifts of the Holy Spirit that we must seek.

—*Homily on the feast of the Holy Prince Daniel of Moscow*
(March 17, 2011)

"True pastoral ministry . . . will be filled with humility and love"

296 "If someone is caught in a sin, you who live by the Spirit should restore that person gently. But watch yourselves, or you also may be tempted" (Gal 6.1). . . . Is it possible to correct and restore a sinner while acting in a spirit of meekness? Indeed, sin is inherent in those who are strong, too, even the strongest ones, so how can a strong man hear the voice of a meek one?

In these apostolic words from Galatians, strange at first glance, lies the greatest wisdom. Those who rectify human sins—the pastors of the Church—should be the first to heed this wisdom. Indeed, the faithful come to them for the confession of their sins and we should put these people right. How often we hear this or that priest severely condemning our sins; how often the faithful encounter utterly irreconcilable and tough mentoring! Sometimes such mentoring even enslaves the human will.

There is no meekness in this kind of mentoring and it does not help the repentant sinner to heal, either. It is only possible to rectify human sins by acting with a spirit of love of the sinner. Why is this? In teaching and correcting another, a meek man will always remember his own sins first of all. When one hears about a sin of the other, how then can one recklessly condemn this poor man while remembering one's own sins? True pastoral ministry, mentorship, and rectification of sins are possible only when the priest, letting the groans of a repentant sinner go through his own heart, responds to him as one remembering his own sins. Then his counsel will never be given in a spirit of power or suppression. It will be filled with humility and love.

—*Homily on the feast of St Seraphim of Vyritsa* (April 3, 2009)

"And whoever of you desires to be first shall be slave of all" (Mk 10.44)

297 The authorities have no function other than to serve. The higher an official is on the service ladder and the more power he has, the more inner humility he will need and the more he should be aware of the obligation to use his position for people's benefit. This is true not only for those who have political power, but also for those who have economic power. It is true for the rich, because wealth is always power. If a person has means exceeding the amount he needs for his own life, it means that God has entrusted him with a special responsibility for others. Doing good works is not an option for a rich man but a requirement, if he wishes for his wealth not to ruin his soul. Similarly, for those who wield political power, the requirement to serve other people constitutes the only proper and God-defined understanding of power.

What we say about power and wealth has a direct bearing on the ecclesial power structure as well. This is all the more true in the Church! Every kind of power given to a person should be accompanied by service, and the higher a person ascends on the stairs of church authority, the more sacrificial his service should be. In this way, the one who is entrusted by God with power over others can be justified. . . . For there is no way to use one's power to impact the soul of another effectively, other than to convey warm thoughts and wishes and to pray with the other, with all love and humility.

—*Homily on the feast of St Seraphim of Vyritsa* (April 3, 2009)

"One flock and one shepherd" (Jn 10.16)

298 Our shepherd the Savior has many sheep. These sheep belong to various pastures, but they all need to be led to the heavenly kingdom. The Lord says that there is only one shepherd, and he will have one flock (Jn 10.16). When we think about the multitude of different traditions existing in Christianity today and about the divisions present in the Christian milieu, we certainly lament the weakening of the one flock of Christ. At the same time, however, we hope that the words of Christ will be realized in history. We do not know yet when it will happen, but we believe that the Lord mysteriously will lead people to this goal of unity. He prayed that we would be one flock, cooperating to safeguard the truth, without which the human race cannot exist.

—*Homily on the feast of St Jonah, Metropolitan of Moscow and All Russia* (June 28, 2010)

"Seek first the kingdom of God and His righteousness" (Mt 6.33)

299 The heavenly kingdom is like a treasure hidden in a field, and somebody finds it and remains silent about finding the treasure. Then he goes and sells everything he has and buys the field in order to dig up this treasure. Similarly, the heavenly kingdom is like a merchant who looks for a precious pearl, and when he finds it, he sells everything he has in order to buy it (Mt 13.44–46). What wonderful images the Savior offers, in order that we may understand what the heavenly kingdom is, a world built on love! It is so beautiful that nothing can be compared to this divine beauty. In order to enter this kingdom, we cannot love God with a small portion, giving him a certain modest part of our attention while using all of our time and resources to achieve other goals we set ourselves. Some may ask, "Is it likely that one can give up everything?" But the Lord does not demand that we should give up everything materially. He demands the only thing—that this kingdom of God should be the dominant, basic principle of life. And if this kingdom of God becomes the ultimate goal and value of our life, then all the rest will come in due course (cf. Mt 6.33).

—*Homily on the feast of St Job, the Patriarch of Moscow and All Russia* (July 2, 2010)

"A royal priesthood" (1 Pet 2.9)

300 The apostolic Church keeps the faith of the holy apostles and proclaims this faith to the whole world. This faith is proclaimed not only by the successors of the apostles, the bishops, not only by clergy ordained by the bishops, but by all the people of God who through baptism and anointing also enter into that which St Peter called the royal priesthood. And the first apostle says these wonderful words addressed to all the faithful: "But you are a chosen generation, a royal priesthood, a holy nation, his own special people" (1 Pet 2.9). You are called to proclaim God's truth as people taken in his possession.

Therefore, the apostolic ministry is our common service. As one Christian community we are all called to keep the apostolic faith and to proclaim it, despite the hardships that the Church continually encounters on her path in history.

—Homily on the feast of the Apostles Peter and Paul (July 12, 2008)

Love and Unity: *"there is no other way"*

301 The Church is called to be the place in which people acquire an experience of love and unity. But where there is division, there is no love. How hypocritical and awful it is when a division occurs in the Church in the name of "lofty" goals! This division is the most dreadful thing that can be experienced in the life of a Christian, because it is the absence of love.

How then can there be the preaching of love? Where then is Christ, if—for the sake of private interests and a particular understanding of aims and tasks on a temporal level—the basis of human existence is destroyed, and love is trampled by human anger? It is a distortion of the Christian message; it is a rejection of the gospel, which is not human but a divine revelation. It is a denial of the gospel with its eternal system of values, which are far from our empty aspirations.

The Church proclaims to those who are near and who are far: there is no other way for the development of the world and human civilization except for the law of love and the way of solidarity, mutual support, harmony, and peace stemming from love.

—Homily on the feast of the Great Prince Vladimir (July 28, 2009)

"How unsearchable are his judgments" (Rom 11.33)

302 " 'For my thoughts are not your thoughts, neither are your ways my ways,' says the Lord" (Is 55.8). It is hard for us to understand God's plan, for God is immeasurably great in relation to the human person. . . . Why would God need the entire drama of human history with its rising and falling, its joys and suffering? The human mind is unable to grasp this. Then what are we left with? We are left only with the need to believe in God and live according to his law. He who has faith and is baptized will be saved (cf. Mk 16.16).

What clear and simple words! . . . Closeness to God at a certain deep spiritual level resolves all the misunderstandings and temptations that sometimes emerge from human attempts at understanding wisdom. It is in the depths of religious experience that we find answers. These are not rational answers, but answers at the level of the heart and our whole life and being. Therefore, in realizing that the divine way and plan of providence is hidden from the human person, we are to put our trust in God, applying this trust in the real categories of our lives. We are to learn how to live according to God's will and endeavor never to violate this will.

—"A Pastor's Word," the patriarch's TV program (2003)

"It is always impossible to exchange God for anything else"

303 The remarkable parable of those called to the feast (Lk 14.16–24) helps us to understand how we must live in order to be with God. To be with God means to follow the path of spiritual perfection, the end of which is human sanctity. . . . And why does this gospel reading help us to understand what is perhaps the most important thing that should be borne in mind for those who wish to ascend the ladder of perfection? This gospel very

clearly states that God ought to be the dominant basis of one's life. It is always impossible to exchange God for anything else. Our bonds of prayer and communion with him are the greatest value of human life, for God is the fount of life. He is the genesis of the human race, human history, and the existence of the whole cosmos, and there is no greater experience than that of communion with God.

We ought not to interpret this parable to mean that the Savior condemns the purchase of land or five pairs of oxen, or the act of marriage. The man who held the feast does not say that it is bad that you have bought land, that you should not have bought any oxen, and that you should not have gotten married. There are no such words in the gospel! But the Lord sets out the priorities and says: in acquiring land, in working upon it, in receiving an education, bringing up children, building yourself a home, and pursuing a career, never forget that the most important thing is to respond to the divine invitation to become participants in the wedding feast! Always respond to God's call to be with him, believe in him, and submit one's life to this faith.

—*Homily on the Sunday of the Holy Forefathers*
(December 25, 2011)

"These men who have turned the world upside down" (Acts 17.6)

304 Everyone who in moments of difficulty feels his faith weaken should recall the holy apostles. . . . Where was the Lord in the life of the apostles? How did he help them? The answer is remarkably simple. He did not save them from violent deaths. He did not protect them from human snares and from natural disasters. It would appear, then, that he did not help them at all. But what was the result of all this? The result of all their trials and challenges was simply this: these unfortunate men, rejected by society, turned the world upside down!

We may ask, haven't there been others throughout the history of the human race with a similar fate? Yes. Were they the only ones to die for an idea? No. Yet where then are the fruits of the endeavors of others who have suffered? We do not know. The fruits of the apostles' lives of suffering and their blessed martyrs' deaths are known by the whole world. . . . Let us pray that the Lord strengthen our faith in our sufferings, lest we weaken when our physical and spiritual strength weaken.

—*Homily on the feast of the Holy Apostles Peter and Paul*
(July 12, 2016)

Prayer and Repentance

305 If every day we turn to God with a prayer for the forgiveness of our sins, opening our heart to God rather than automatically repeating a memorized text, and if we humbly present to the Lord's judgment what is going on in the depths of our soul, it will mean that we live a religious life. At first this prayer of repentance may seem tiresome, even though it takes only a few minutes, but when it becomes a habit, you will no longer come out in the street or begin your day without it. . . . Our faith, continually subjected to various temptations and pressures from outside, becomes stronger when we acquire an experience of repentance.

—*Sermon on the feast of the Beheading of John the Baptist*
(September 11, 2015)

Becoming Human

306 Wherever there is suffering, there opens up within the human person a special vision and ability to see God, and a special

strength and ability to feel the divine presence in life. This does not mean that everyone has to endure suffering, but it does mean that the person who does not have to undergo this suffering ought to cleanse his soul through his good deeds and through participation in the suffering of his neighbor. . . . We become human beings when we retain the ability to do good deeds.

—*Speech at the Center for Medical Aid to Children* (January 7, 2012)

"The meaning and goal of our lives"

307 Christ founded the Church in order to reveal within her the meaning and goal of our lives: why we are here, what can we hope for, what we are to do. And he reveals to us that we are created for everlasting and blessed life, and that these few decades of our earthly path are a very important time to prepare for eternity, when we will reap the fruits of the labors that we have accomplished here on earth. This eternity may be endlessly joyful, blessed, and comforting; on the other hand, alas, it may not be such. The Lord founded the Church for one purpose only—to bring his eternal salvation to all.

When people awaken to this and strive for eternal salvation, earthly life changes: drunkards abandon their vices; criminals become honest citizens; people who are despondent and lost find strength and cheer. The person who has belief in the Savior and in salvation is capable of enduring with patience and hope that which another may not be able to endure, for he sees before himself eternal and not temporary perspectives. He becomes a different person altogether and his system of values is transformed. He finds the true goal of and true joy in his life. What before seemed important and valuable, and that which he was prepared to do anything for (even committing a crime), becomes worthless and unnecessary. God created the human person for eternal joy and blessedness. We must remember this.

—*"Patriarch Kirill: Spiritual life is not a hobby for which we may or may not have enough time," interview with the magazine* Foma (May 6, 2013)

The Problem of Evil

308 Some people, when thinking upon the subject of suffering, begin to protest against God and say: how can we call God the loving Father if there is so much suffering in the world, so much injustice, so many diseases, and so many premature deaths, including the deaths of innocent children? How can we reconcile this with divine love and divine omnipotence? . . .

If we attempt to solve the problem of human suffering within the framework of human life, then we waste our time. Moreover, if we base our outlook on life solely on those years that God has given us for our sojourn on earth, we will never arrive at a coherent understanding of the meaning of human life. Everything turns into a sort of madness. We live sixty, seventy, eighty years, and then we cease to live. What has it all meant? What is the meaning of these decades, if they have meaning at all? If we reject God and reject eternity, then there is no meaning, but all is vanity of vanities and despondency of spirit, as the wise Solomon said (Eccl 1.14). . . . In whatever conditions of the confines of our earthly and physical existence we find ourselves, we know that suffering and affliction will surely come, no matter how great and powerful the human person becomes.

Yet for God there is no dividing line between the earthly world and the spiritual world. If we perceive our existence in the perspective of eternity, then it is on the scale of eternity that human grief and affliction are overcome. Our short-lived, almost momentary sojourn in the physical body here on earth, which passes by so quickly, as those who are older know, is filled with meaning. Meaning is revealed in eternity, and in eternity all the terrible questions on reconciling divine love and human suffering are resolved, for the hungry there receive food, the thirsty receive water, and the afflicted rejoice.

Some may object that we can combat all of this trouble in this world. Yet perhaps we should just hope that all afflictions and illnesses will be overcome after death? The Lord gives us amazing examples that those who place themselves in the hands of God and who live according to God's commandments and laws acquire great strength of spirit, capable of reducing all affliction and grief to ash.

—*Homily on the feast of Sts Sergius and Herman, the* Wonderworkers *of Valaam* (July 11, 2014)

"Speaking the truth in love" (Eph 4.15)

309 The Church's word is always replete with love, for the Lord himself brought us his love. This is why the Church became a healing community in the direct sense of the word, for it is in the Church that the Savior's ministry is continued, in particular for the physical healing of people. But more than this, the Church is called a healing community because she is called to heal the wounded souls of people and society. The sole means of their healing is love.

With love, the Church preaches Christ to the world, even if the world is incapable of receiving this word with love. The Church has no other weapon. She does not have the right to use force, and indeed she has no force. What force can there be in earthly ashes? The Church has no other means of affecting people's consciousness than through her preaching, filled with love and righteousness. Yet how important this mission is for the entire human race! Even if her preaching goes against the general current of life, with its false and dangerous values, how important it is that this preaching be heard!

—*Homily on the feast of the Synaxis of the Twelve Apostles* (July 13, 2009)

"In Jesus Christ God has adopted us"

310 Christ has given to us the possibility of addressing God as "Father" and "Abba." He has taught us an amazing prayer, the Lord's Prayer, or the Our Father. Yet do we have the right to address God so boldly? Yes, we do, for in Jesus Christ God has adopted us. He truly is the heavenly Father. Christ is indeed the Son of God, and in him all that is human has been united with the divine. This means that through Christ, all people are united with God the Father. "As it is impossible to see with our eyes without light or speak without a tongue . . . then it is impossible for the human person to be saved and enter into the kingdom of heaven without the Lord Jesus" (St Ephraim the Syrian).

If God is our Father, then we are his children. This means that each person is tied to other people in the same way that brothers and sisters are joined through the bonds of kinship. Our ideal human relationships should be brotherly. This is why, on the path to union with God, we are called to transform our lives and the lives of those around us in a special way. This special world and order of existence is called in Scripture the kingdom of God. It was this that the Savior came to proclaim. The kingdom of God is life in communion with God the Father through Jesus Christ in the Holy Spirit.

Christian faith calls people to love each other and on the foundation of love to build up a brotherly relationship, so that all together may be in communion with the one God the Father, by whom we are adopted through his divine Son Jesus Christ, who has enabled us to partake of the Holy Spirit. Through the power of the Spirit of God, we are also capable of attaining the goal of existence: to participate in building up the kingdom of God and entering into it here on earth, so that we may possess it in full measure in eternity.

—*A Pastor's Word* (Moscow: DECR, 2008), 404–406

"So then it is not of him who wills, nor of him who runs, but of God who shows mercy" (Rom 9.16)

311 "For by grace you have been saved through faith, and that not of yourselves; it is the gift of God, not of works, lest any one should boast" (Eph 2.8–9). . . . People will ask: "Is it really impossible to be a good person and at the same time a non-believer? Is it really necessary, in order to do good deeds, that I go to church?" We reply: "Of course it is possible to be a good person and do good deeds as a non-believer. But we cannot save our own soul!" The kingdom of God cannot be acquired in the soul without faith and without divine grace. Without faith, we can be decent and good human beings, but we cannot overcome sin within ourselves without the power of the grace of God.

Herein lies the whole meaning of the epistle which the Church today addresses to the world. Of course, it is better to be good than evil. There are many good people who are well brought up and want only good, yet who are not believers. And if the human person, relying on his upbringing, on family and other traditions, is able to develop within himself good qualities, then thank God! Yet this person should know that while he is close to the kingdom of God, truly only a short distance away from it, he won't be able to cross the threshold of this kingdom without the power of divine grace. The Lord called not "the righteous, but sinners to repentance" (Mt 9.13; Mk 2.17). Yet the word of God is also addressed to good, well intentioned people, calling upon them to open up their hearts to God, to receive his power, energy, and grace as the means to transformation of one's inner world and the attainment of the kingdom of God.

—*Homily on Saturday of the First Week of Lent* (March 7, 2009)

"There is no partiality with God" (Rom 2.11)

312 All human differences are our differences, our conditions. But when we leave this life to go to the Lord, we will take our place among others, regardless of our rank or position, spiritual or secular, and humbly wait our turn to be judged, since for God there are no human differences. Understanding this helps the Christian to be always humble and to discharge his duty honorably no matter what this duty may be: whether that of a ruler, an army officer, a bishop, or simply that of the individual. We should constantly recall that no honor linked to high position will ever overshadow the great truth that we are all equal before God. And this awareness should fill us with a feeling of genuine humility.

—*Homily on Great and Holy Thursday* (April 16, 2009)

How to Avoid Judging Others

313 The word of God warns us of inevitable punishment for the sin of judging. It clearly testifies that our human judgment will turn in the future into God's particular judgment in relation to ourselves. "For with what judgment you judge, you will be judged" (Mt 7.2). And when we stand before the Lord, the more often we have allowed ourselves here on earth to make human judgment, which is iniquitous and unjust, the more severe will be God's judgment on us.

What then are we to do in order to guard ourselves from this vice? We are to constantly remind ourselves of our own sinful nature. As soon as we feel the desire to condemn someone, it is essential to recall the sins that weigh down our souls. Each of us carries a baggage from these heavy recollections. As we look upon the person we were about to judge, let us ask ourselves: can I, with my heavy load, with my burdened conscience, condemn him? St John Climacus has taught us: "Never be ashamed of the one before you who says evil things to his neighbor, but better to say to him: 'Cease, brother, for daily I fall into the worst sins and how can I judge?' In this manner you will accomplish two good things and with a single plaster heal both yourself and your neighbor. This is one of the shortest paths to receiving forgiveness of sins, that is, never condemning anyone."[14]

—*Homily on Tuesday of the First Week of Lent* (February 16, 2010)

"*Godmanhood has broken down the barrier between God and the human person*"

314 God loves us! This fundamental religious truth with great power is revealed in Godmanhood.[15] In the Old Testament, God appears to people as the Creator of the universe, the omnipotent protector of the chosen people and its awesome teacher. In the New Testament, God appears in the flesh by becoming the Son of Man, a carpenter by the name of Jesus from the town of Nazareth. This manifestation of God in the flesh is the great and wonderful revelation of divine love. When we connect with the mystery of this love, we do away with all questions about the extreme, inscrutable nature of the Savior's sacrifice for our corrupted human race. God's infinite love for us explains all things and embraces all things.

[14]John Climacus, *Oration* 10.7.

[15]The word "Godmanhood" (*Bogochelovechestvo*) was popularized by the Russian thinkers Vladimir Solovyov (1853–1900), Nikolai Berdyaev (1874–1948), and Sergius Bulgakov (1871–1944). Patriarch Kirill uses the word to refer to the Church's teaching on the incarnation of the Son of God and the deification of man.

In being free to choose our way in life, we have the chance to respond to this divine love through our love, so that we may abide in union and unity with our Savior. God loved us and loves us more than our kinsmen in the flesh and those closest to us. And this means that Godmanhood has broken down the barrier between God and the human person, uniting the divine and human natures in the one person of Christ. Through him, we can turn to our Creator, calling him Father.

—*A Pastor's Word* (Moscow: DECR, 2008), 84–85

"The unity of the Spirit in the bond of peace" (Eph 4.3)

315 Our outer witness will be effective when we have love and oneness in the Church. Therefore, we are to strengthen the unity of Holy Orthodoxy and the Orthodox churches in all ways possible. The lives of the people who are pastorally cared for by the local churches are greatly varied, for there are a multitude of various cultures in the world, and political, social, and economic conditions are formed in different ways. All of this influences the worldview of people, and the contradictions of the modern world—whether we like it or not—are transported into relationships between the churches. This is why our ability to preserve the unity of the entire Orthodox Church depends on the hierarchs of the churches, on the episcopate, the clergy, and the faithful. We are obliged in all ways possible to strengthen the unity of Holy Orthodoxy.

—*Homily on the feast of the Dormition of the Mother of God*
   (August 28, 2016)

"Work out your own salvation . . . for it is God who works in you" (Phil 2.12–13)

316 Fasting, prayer, and good deeds are the means by which we prepare our souls for receiving divine grace. We are saved by grace, but without our efforts grace is ineffectual. If we do not make an effort, then the partaking of the holy mysteries of Christ will be not for the salvation of our souls, but "for judgment and condemnation." It was pleasing to God that our salvation be accomplished not only through his power but also with our participation. And our participation is expressed in our attempts to limit the sinful strivings of our nature, to enter into prayerful communion with God, and to learn how to interact with each other by being bonded tightly together through charity. Our salvation is accomplished in the Church by the power of grace in response to our human endeavors.

—*Homily on Saturday of the First Week of Lent* (March 7, 2009)

"They have given me more than I may have given them"

317 Loneliness develops when a person has no object of love. If there is an object of love, loneliness disappears. And what is the absence of an object of love? It is an absence of another person to whom you can convey your inner feelings and show your attention, concern, and love. Our individualism, egoism, and self-isolation are the cause of our loneliness. . . .

The way out of this tragic condition is very simple. Let's look more closely at who is around us and how many people today need our care and our attention. I love to visit the elderly, lonely, and disabled, especially on Christmas and Pascha. Sometimes I am asked, "You have come once already, so perhaps this is sufficient?" I reply, "I don't come so that the TV can show how nice the Patriarch is. I come out of my inner need. When I visit the poor and elderly, I come out a different man. I feel how my soul has become brighter. It is the same feeling you have after a divine service. Indeed, we know that people come out of a church with a light heart. I leave these people feeling the same. They have given me more than I may have given them."

So I would suggest to everyone who suffers from loneliness to go into the world with a good and open heart and come to those who need help. One such visit can help you find friends and kindred spirits and an object of your care, breaking your loneliness.

—*Interview on Nativity for the TV channel* Russia-1
(January 7, 2014)

"The strength of the Christian"

318 Christ's cross teaches us to accept suffering with humility. Of course, we cannot pretend that nothing is wrong when life delivers harsh blows to us, but these blows should not break our will, destroy our lives, or impact who we are as people. We are to convert all things to good: the failures in our lives and the illnesses and pain that God sends us, remembering that if the Lord allowed suffering for the sake of our salvation, then our pain has saving meaning for us.

The strength of the Christian lies first of all in this: by placing his hope in God's will and trusting in God, he is able resolutely and without protest to vanquish pain and suffering, and so be inwardly strong and invincible. The Savior looks down upon us from the cross and calls upon every one of us to follow his example and bear our own crosses. This will open up to us the doors of salvation, making us stronger, wiser, and more spiritually elevated. All of this is possible through a Christian approach to our cross, pain, and suffering. The Lord gives us not only an example, but also strength. When, from the depths of the misfortune that has befallen us, we turn our gaze and ardent prayer toward him, then in response to this God grants us strength to overcome our trials.

—*Homily on the eve of the Third Sunday of Lent* (March 21, 2009)

"*Ministry as a sacrifice*"

319 Not possession or a power trip, but ministry and service— this is what distinguishes our understanding of authority in the Church. This is what Christ commanded his disciples to do. Do you recall when he washed their feet and explained why he did this (Jn 13.14–15)? He who wants to be first should be the servant of all! I view my patriarchal ministry as a sacrifice that should be offered to God and people every day. . . . If those of us in the Church hierarchy grow, it should be in the increase of self-sacrifice and self-surrender, and not at all in the possession of privileges by those in charge. This is an unconstrained and freely offered sacrifice, and I would even say that it is joyful and full of gratitude.

—"*By Denying Divine Truth We Ruin the World,*" *an interview with the news agency TASS* (March 10, 2015)

The Cure for the Disease of Busyness

320 The problem of time is the problem of our inner condition. We truly are all the time heading off to some new destination, and feel we have a catastrophic lack of time. We are certainly busy, expending an enormous amount of energy in our pursuits. It often happens that one builds up momentum all one's life with ceaseless activity, and then suddenly circumstances conspire so that we fall ill and become derailed and are forced to stop.

And then we begin to think: what have I achieved? Yes, I've acquired a bigger apartment and I have a new car. . . . But what have I achieved—what have I left for posterity? When we expend a huge amount of effort toward material gain, it is the same thing as running in place. And in order not to get on this treadmill, like a squirrel running round at tremendous speed but getting nowhere, we have to learn how to stop.

Prayer is the means by which we can stop. When one turns to God, one enters into a completely different dimension. In prayer, one takes a bird's eye view of one's life and realizes: "O Lord, all of this is vanity of vanities, this isn't what is most important!" Prayer helps one to set one's priorities in life and come to a state of tranquility so that one can cope with stress.

—*Interview for the TV channel* Russia-1 (September 21, 2010)

"Believers both by conviction and our way of life"

321 The power of the Church's preaching is based not only and not so much on the power of conviction. It is based on a living and real experience of people who can share this experience with those both near and far. That is why it is so important that our religiosity, at times more closely resembling something cultural rather than genuinely religious—more about our outer respectability rather than about a true inner life—changes, so that we become believers both by conviction and our way of life. Only this type of person is capable of being true to the cross "even unto death" (Phil 2.8).

—*Homily on Friday of the Fourth Week of Lent* (April 1, 2011)

"Every believer ought to transmit the light of truth"

322 To whom is the Savior's appeal addressed to teach and baptize all nations (cf. Matt 28.16–20)? Was he speaking only to his disciples? No, indeed, he is addressing all his followers, both those who have received apostolic ministry from the hands of the apostles and all of those people who believe in Christ.

It is important to understand that if we confess ourselves to be believers, then we ought to recall that "faith working through love" (Gal 5.6) is in its nature active. It is not enough to believe: every believer is called to convey his faith to others and share with them his spiritual treasure. That is why the words uttered by the Lord to the eleven apostles are at the same time addressed to all the members of the Church. Every believer ought to transmit the light of truth to at least one non-believer in order to share with him the joy of confessing Jesus Christ.

—*A Pastor's Word* (Moscow: DECR, 2008), 381

"Faith is a gift of God"

323 Why does one person believe and another not? Faith is a gift of God and it is sent down upon people without exception. However, some are able to receive it, while others are not, for there are certain moral conditions for the human person to assimilate faith in God. Of course, it would be a mistake to suggest that only virtuous people have a special ability to believe. A great sinner can also believe, if only he has not ceased to discern the accusing voice of his conscience, and then, like the tax collector of the Lord's parable, he sees his own sins and repents of them without seeking self-justification.

—*A Pastor's Word* (Moscow: DECR, 2008), 282

Our Gethsemane, Our Golgotha

324 Each of us throughout his life enters his garden of Gethsemane and ascends to his Golgotha. Of course, our Gethsemane and our Golgotha are incommensurate with those of the Lord, for trials are sent to each according to his strength. We have to endure afflictions and fear, longing, despondency, and loneliness.

It may seem that our sufferings are unjust, and that people are incapable of appreciating the good that we have done them or are ready to do for them.

How can we help ourselves to achieve harmony of the spiritual and the material, the temporal and the eternal? How are we to overcome the weakness of our human nature? We do this by following the example of the Lord, who surrendered himself in the Garden of Gethsemane to the mercy of the heavenly Father and the saving providence of God, uttering in meekness: "Not as I will, but as you will" (Mt 26.39).

If we learn how to submit our wills at the most difficult moments in life to the divine will and submit our human principle to the divine principle, we will live and act as the Lord commanded us to do. In this we will acquire an inner harmony and strength of spirit, as our Savior found them as he prayed, neglected and lonely, in the garden of Gethsemane.

—A *Pastor's Word* (Moscow: DECR, 2008), 340–341

Readings for Feast Days

Selected Fixed Feast Days

The Presentation of the Theotokos

325 The heavenly queen began her life journey with the temple. . . . There, in the temple in Jerusalem, she was brought up and educated. There she went from strength to strength (Ps 83.7). Her remarkable inherent qualities, strengthened by God's grace and her good will, unfolded there, bringing abundant fruits. . . . We need the guidance of God's grace in everything, in private life and in spiritual growth, as it was with the Virgin Mary at the Jerusalem temple.

We also need the guidance of God's grace in the solution of social and political problems and in the improvement of our human relations, the more so in the improvement of our country. We need the churches of God to help us learn to feel deeply and to be transformed people who are fully aware of what God's presence means. The Church helps us to reconcile with ourselves, with our conscience, and with people around us; through her, we are strengthened and become capable of defending God's truth in this world, and able to improve this world together with God. The Church is given to us so that we might feed on the divine grace so strongly present there. God's grace is capable of transforming our personality and our life according to God's design for the world and man.

—*Homily on the feast of the Entry of the Theotokos into the Temple* (December 4, 2009)

Nativity

326 The Incarnation of the Son of God, or Nativity, was an act of boundless, divine love. God made the law of love the basis for the world and then lived out the truth of this law himself in the life of Jesus Christ. Christ's life on this earth manifested God's love, which knows no bounds or limits, even when it must undergo unbearable sufferings and death. Jesus' love wasn't limited to a small set of relatives, friends, or like-minded men. Rather, it extended to those who persecuted, tortured, and crucified him— those we would designate as enemies. An enemy is not the one who hates us, but the one whom we designate as an enemy, one born in our minds and in our hearts.

Christ had no enemies. For him, all humanity consisted of brothers and sisters who had gone astray and whom he came to save. On Christmas night, divine love entered the world as a newborn baby, vulnerable and defenseless, born not in a royal palace but in the squalid cave where the shepherds kept their sheep in bad weather. The great mystery is contained within this picture of Christmas: the salvation of the world comes neither from riches nor strength nor power, but from that love which exceeds any human strength by its vulnerability and defenselessness.

—*Nativity Message* (January 7, 1991)

The Synaxis of the Theotokos

327 Today we remember the family of the Savior. By this mere remembrance the Church emphasizes the importance of family and family relations, and of bearing children and togetherness, especially in the face of hardship and danger. It is so important to support each other and share what we can with each other, first and foremost with the members of our family! For often love disappears when we stop sharing with others, and then we get estranged and family bonds break.

That is why today we pray for families. We pray for members of our families; we pray that children will be born into them, that mass murders of unborn infants will stop, that the birth of every child would bring great happiness as relatives become closer and feel the importance of each other. Of course, today we also pray for our children, for whom unknown paths will lead to the future, the end of the twenty-first century. It is difficult to imagine what that time will be like, and our children will have to take the Orthodox faith and fidelity to Christ and his divine law with them to that distant future.

That is why the Church lifts up her fervent prayers for parents and children and for our families. We believe that by our prayers, feeble though they are, the Lord will show his mercy both to the parents and to the children, helping them perceive, among other things, the great wisdom that has been passed on to us by the holy Scripture cherished in the Church.

—*Homily on the Synaxis of the Most Holy Theotokos*
(January 8, 2015)

Theophany

328 We know that sin divides God and the human person, the Creator and creation. The baptism of Christ, Epiphany, was a sign of God's presence in the world and in human history. Through Jesus Christ, the wall that divides God and the human person was destroyed. God became a human person of one essence with human nature, thus uniting himself with this world. Henceforth, divine grace and power abide in our world abundantly. When on the feast of Christ's baptism we bless water, we thereby testify to the great truth of the pervasive and saving presence of divine energy in the physical nature of our world. Holy water is the great symbol of the presence of God's grace in the life of the universe.

—*A Pastor's Word* (Moscow: DECR, 2008), 115

The Meeting of the Lord in the Temple

329 God bestowed upon us his presence in history not only through his Son our Lord Jesus Christ. The Lord bestowed upon us his presence in our lives through his word, through his thoughts, and through his teaching. When we read the gospel and meditate upon the words uttered by the Lord, we encounter his divine thoughts, ideas and teaching. And when we see these ideas, these thoughts, these words embodied in our lives, we truly encounter the Lord. Therefore our encounters with radiant, pure people who live according to God's commandments are likened to an encounter with God, since the divine truth is embodied in these people.

When we come into contact with beauty and harmony in the world, with that which is the result of the divine plan for the world and the human person, we also encounter God. When we see nature in her beauty, or the greatness of human creative design come to fruition, whether it be in art, music, literature, architecture, or in any way that beauty is revealed to the world, we also encounter God. For God is the source of harmony and beauty.

—*Homily on the Meeting of the Lord* (February 15, 2001)

Transfiguration I: God's Energies Transfigure the World

330 In old icons that depict the event of the Transfiguration of the Lord, we see Christ standing on the mountaintop while the apostles in reverent awe are prostrate before the great miracle that the Savior has shown them. From the figure of the Lord, blinding streams of golden light emerge in all directions. This is God's gracious energy, penetrating the surrounding mountains, trees, rocks, and people, as it fills the whole of God's world and the entirety of creation. This iconographic image contains a remarkably profound theological idea: the inexhaustible divine energy of our God and Creator permeates the whole world and transfigures it. The life of the human person is also upheld by the saving action of God's grace. This is the only power in the world capable of transforming us by calling us forth into the light, out of the darkness of error and mistakes, failures and despair.

—*A Pastor's Word* (Moscow: DECR, 2008), 244

Transfiguration II: Transfiguration and Christ's Crucifixion

331 God, eternal and inscrutable, dwelling where we cannot be because of our physical nature, is always beside us. The Lord gave the vision of his closeness to people on Mt Tabor. It was not accidental that the Savior revealed his glory and divine nature to his disciples, showing them ahead of his passion and suffering that he was the Son of God.

It was not accidental that the disciples witnessed Christ's transformation and experienced the closeness of God to them. This was done to make the Jewish people see that at the moment when the teacher was taken up to the cross, disgraced and profaned, when his mission was trampled and abased in their eyes—at that very moment of shame and defeat, they could see in the powerless man's dead body the mysterious and salvific presence of God.

—*Homily on the feast of the Transfiguration of the Lord* (August 19, 2011)

Dormition

332 The Most Holy Mother of God cleansed the inner expanse of her soul in her heart so that the Lord could enter into this expanse by filling it with his grace and with himself. The virgin became the mother of the Son of God, the Lord Jesus Christ, the one who made himself felt mainly through his humility.

In full measure we are aware of how difficult it is for today's person to receive a word on humility. Today's person finds it much easier to receive completely different words. Yet can life according to the law of one's ego, in which one is striving for the constant gratification of one's needs and the complete exclusion of others from one's life, really bring us happiness? . . . The humble person bears within himself the constant potential for happiness independent of life's circumstances. In spite of his position in life, the humble person always has joy in his heart, for God is with him and divine grace is with him, which means that so, too, is the fullness of life. The humble person is always happy, even if outwardly he may not seem so. The example of the queen of Heaven and Virgin Mary is the unfading ideal for every Christian.

—*Homily on the feast of the Dormition of the Theotokos*
   (August 28, 2014)

Triodion, Great Lent, Holy Week, Pascha, Paschaltide

Sunday of Zacchaeus

333 Today we have read the beginning of the Gospel of St Luke about the conversion of Zacchaeus (Lk 19.1–10). . . . This passage teaches us many things. Each of us commits sins, and the higher one's position, the more often one's sins make an impact on other people. By our sins we always offend others, be they our colleagues, our husbands, or our wives. Sin always brings misfortune, though it sometimes seems that it sits so deeply in us that nobody can discern it. Hidden or not, sin always destroys the sinner himself and brings misfortune to other people.

The example of Zacchaeus teaches us that however sinful each of us may be, however heavy the load lying on our heart may be, we have an opportunity to draw God's love and mercy to us. And we do not have to climb up trees; we should simply be determined, like Zacchaeus was, to confess before God our intention to forgive other people and to return to them what was unjustly taken from them, be it material valuables or something else. We must commit to share our lives with people, giving them a part of ourselves. Then we will hear the remarkable words of salvation that the Lord spoke to Zacchaeus.

—*Homily on the Sunday of Zacchaeus* (January 17, 2010)

The Sunday of the Publican and the Pharisee

334 This Sunday we are reflecting on the Parable of the Publican and the Pharisee that the Lord told to His disciples. . . .

What does this text teach us? As St Theophan the Recluse remarkably put it, "Being zealous in virtue (that is, striving to do good), pin all your hopes on the Lord, for it is he who saves." St Theophan did not say that good works are worthless. He suggested that we should be zealous in virtue, that is, strive to do good, but remember that the Lord is the one who saves us. We might ask, what saves man? Where does salvation begin? The answer is in today's parable. The publican, aware of his sinfulness and appealing to God, does not say, "Lord, now I will go out and start paying the tithe and doing good works." He does not say that. He implores God to show his mercy to him, a sinner. He knows that he is a sinner and is perishing. He knows how important for him this prayer and this yearning for God are, and he addresses him with these simple words, "God, be merciful to me, a sinner."

Here is the beginning of our salvation. If we think that our good works, our customary way of life, and our observance of the laws both state and ecclesiastical might save us, we are wrong. . . . If we are not aware of our sinfulness and of the fact that it is God who saves, and if we have no repentance, then no good works will save us. They will always be some kind of falsehood that prevents us from seeing the depth of our fall and sinfulness.

—*Homily on the Sunday of the Publican and the Pharisee*
  (February 24, 2013)

The Parable of the Prodigal Son

335 We are reflecting on the parable of the Prodigal Son today, on the threshold of Lent, which is a special period in the life of every man. Fasting is given to us so that we can pray and ponder over our life, deeds, and thoughts, and bring them to the impartial court of our conscience while praying to God that he forgive our transgressions and release us from the captivity of sin. May the parable of the Prodigal Son become for all of us a great source of hope that God will forgive us, deliver us from sins, and help us find peace and joy in communion with him in his Father's house.

—*Homily on the Sunday of the Prodigal Son* (February 20, 2011)

Sunday of the Last Judgment

336 How can we ever find justification? After all, we all commit sinful acts in our thoughts and deeds. Today's gospel reading (Mt 25.31–46) helps us to understand what can save us, what can compensate for our faults, and how we can atone for our guilt. Have you fed the hungry? Have you given the thirsty something to drink? Have you received a stranger? Clothed the naked? Visited the sick or those in prison?

How short this list is! It would seem that the Lord, who brought these commandments into the world, ought to have placed them in the mouth of the divine judge: "Did you observe this, that, or the other commandment?" The Lord no longer speaks of commandments; rather, he speaks of concrete deeds. And we know that this list could go on, for it concerns not only the sick, the naked, the hungry, the thirsty, or the prisoners, but also speaks of helping any person.

Why does helping another person redeem our sins? Because it is in this help and in this ability to accomplish good works that the greatest of commandments and the greatest of values is revealed. A person without love in his heart is incapable of doing such things.

Many may say, "I don't feel love, except maybe for my family—my father, mother, brother, sister, wife, and children, and even then. . . ." How are we to acquire this love so that we bring good to people? Not through any artificial will power, not through any ardent desire to love our neighbor, not through any decision to begin loving someone on Monday or after New Year's Day—no, nothing will ever come of this.

Love appears in the heart gradually through good deeds. When we do good deeds for people, we are no longer indifferent to them and they are no longer people far from us, but instead they become our neighbors. The more good deeds we do, the stronger the love in our hearts will grow, because there are no other means and no other possibility of growing in love than in accomplishing those deeds which will be our salvation at the Last Judgment.

—*Homily on the Sunday of the Last Judgment* (March 10, 2013)

Forgiveness Sunday (Cheesefare Sunday)

337 Today's gospel reading contains these remarkable words: "Do not lay up for yourselves treasures on earth, where moth and rust destroy and where thieves break in and steal," for earthly treasure is transient, unfaithful, and can easily lead one to ruin. "But lay up for yourselves treasures in heaven, where neither moth nor rust destroys and where thieves do not break in and steal," the Savior insists. This is said of our earthly lives, that our preferences and our choices indicate where our hearts, wills, and the center of our attention reside. "For where your treasure is, there your heart will be also," concludes the Gospel text (Mt 6.19–21).

If the center of our attention and the treasure of our hearts are life everlasting, goodness, righteousness, and the acquisition of unsurpassed moral values, then we enter eternity with these spiritual riches. But if our hearts are filled to the brim only with what belongs to this world and has worth only in this earthly life, then when we depart for the next world, our earthly treasure will remain the captive of time and corruption, and we will enter eternity with nothing.

Today is the last day before Great Lent begins, and is it not fortuitous that Christians are invited to meditate upon what fasting means? This is a special time of life when we are offered the opportunity and given the means to ever and again concentrate our attention upon unsurpassed values, on the world of the spirit, and on life eternal, to test ourselves in the struggle against falsehood and evil. Not only in the depths of our souls, but also in the active currents of life, we long to taste victory over sin, evil, and falsehood.

—*Homily on Forgiveness Sunday* (March 17, 2002)

"Repentance lies at the heart of our Lenten efforts"

338 Fasting suggests a change of one's mind and heart. In the ancient Greek language, "change" and "repentance" are the same word, *metanoia*. Repentance lies at the heart of our Lenten efforts, and the goal of our fasting is to change and return to God. This is no superficial change, like trying a new style of hair or clothing. This is the transformation of self, with God's help, into a new man fighting against and conquering sins. When we fast, we declare an uncompromising, life-or-death war with sin. For sin kills us as persons and changes us into slaves of passions ruled by the enemy.

—*Interview on Pascha with the Russian Information Agency* Novosty (May 5, 2013)

"Trying to know ourselves"

339 Great Lent is a special time that we are to spend with benefit so that the days—which in fact go by so quickly—do not pass us by. . . . Today many people's lives are so far removed from the Church's ordinances. The cares of this life distract and reorient us toward goals far removed from those goals that we as Orthodox Christians ought to set for ourselves as we set out on our journey through the holy fast. People are busy working, studying, and attending to a huge amount of important or trivial things. . . . In spite of this vanity, during Great Lent we are to try to focus our attention on our spiritual lives.

The fathers teach us that it is at this time, the time of fasting and praying, that we are to focus on trying to know ourselves. The ascetic tradition of the Church tells us that self-knowledge is aimed not at admiring our virtues, our talents, or our success, but on paying attention to our sins.

—*Homily on Tuesday of the First Week of Lent* (February 24, 2015)

Fasting, Repentance, and Forgiveness

340 The aim and meaning of a fast is repentance, the liberation of a person from sin, a change for the better in his or her inner state. The most important thing in a fast is the forgiveness that we receive from God. Repentance that does not end in forgiveness is senseless. Repentance that bears this divine forgiveness is salvific, since the Lord clearly says to us that only those who themselves forgive others can hope for forgiveness. If you do not forgive others, God will not forgive you either.

—*Homily on Monday of the First Week of Lent* (March 14, 2016)

Awareness of Sin and the Path to Healing

341 We must begin our Lenten journey by condemning ourselves, repudiating sin, and expressing our firm intention to oppose "seducing spirits and doctrines of devils" (1 Tim 4.1). It is impossible to achieve genuine repentance if in our subconscious, in the secret corners of our mind and souls, sin still has for us its attraction. Only a clear awareness of sin as corruption and disease, and as the fount of spiritual discord and inevitable spiritual death, can help man be firm in embarking on the path to spiritual healing.

—*Homily on Monday of the First Week of Lent* (February 23, 2004)

Tools for Spiritual Renewal

342 Repentance, fasting, prayer, and charity are the four means for spiritual renewal and moral rebirth. For two thousand years, the faithful of God's Church have had recourse to these tools, and the fact that a multitude of people have found the fullness of life, joy, and peace in faith testifies that this spiritual healing is true.

However, we should also recall that our salvation and our spiritual growth do not happen suddenly in a single instant. A tree does not grow to its full height immediately, a house cannot be built straight away, and the human person does not grow to maturity instantly. . . . Therefore, all of us who undertake spiritual warfare, who repent of our sins, and who fast, pray, and try to accomplish good deeds ought to understand that a long road of hard work awaits us. There is no magic wand by which good changes in our lives and in our spiritual condition are wrought by a single wave. But insofar as repentance, fasting, prayer, and charity are rooted in our lives, then something very important happens to us: zeal for the spiritual life will grow within us.

—*Homily on Wednesday of the First Week of Lent* (March 12, 2003)

"There is still hope"

343 Hope is one of the greatest Christian virtues. Ultimately, it is the belief that God will always help us where our own strength is not enough. If hope has not died within us, if it is fortified by faith and ardent prayer to the Lord, and if we never cease to ask the Lord to help us overcome our sin, then no matter how difficult life's circumstances, how weak our human nature is, or how much we have become accustomed to sin, God can answer our prayer! He helps us to vanquish the sin that has become a part of our nature and entered into our lives at the deepest level. "Then we have only to abandon hope for repentance when we are in hell, for only there is this remedy powerless and of no benefit; while we are here—albeit in old age or even at the gates of death—hope is beneficial and saving," St John Chrysostom teaches us.

It is not at all a coincidence that the Lord calls upon us to forgive unto seventy times seven (Mt 18.22). Indeed, while there is still forgiveness, while there is still repentance, there is still hope for our correction and spiritual transformation. In response to our feat of repentance and because of the power of hope and the power of prayer, God can genuinely change us and free us from the captivity of sin. Therefore, never and in no circumstances should the believer, even the one who abides in sin, ever lose hope in God's mercy.

—*Homily on Tuesday of the First Week of Lent* (February 24, 2004)

Second Sunday of Lent: St Gregory Palamas

344 The mark of the light of divine energy and the grace of Mt Tabor can also be seen on us, though we are common people. Surely we all have happened to meet someone whom we could look in the eyes and say at once, "Such a radiant person; it is so good to be with him!" Likewise, many of us might have met someone, and while looking into his eyes we would think, "What a terrible man!" The appearance reflects man's inward state.

The radiance of the Tabor light was seen on the faces of the Athonite elders. They were called "hesychasts," and this Greek word is still used in our theology and ascetic practice. St Gregory Palamas was a bearer of this hesychast tradition. The spiritual education of St Sergius of Radonezh also had its origins in this tradition during the same period, in the fourteenth century. Many monasteries in Russia were established in accordance with the Athonite monastic order, following the example of St Gregory Palamas and the Athonite monks.

Why do we speak about this on the second Sunday of Lent? It is because the purpose of our fasting is to gain the divine grace that shone so brightly in their lives.

—*Homily on the Second Sunday of Lent* (March 31, 2013)

Third Sunday of Lent: Veneration of the Cross

345 The cross is undoubtedly an affliction, but by the will and design of God, this affliction becomes saving when we overcome it. We grow spiritually as we overcome affliction. I have occasion to speak with parents whose children are underdeveloped or suffer from physical diseases that make them different from other children, and I have noticed the various reactions of parents to these things. Some are crushed by grief and there is a hollow look in their faces, and life as they knew it has come to an end. But I have also seen parents with radiant faces inclined over the child or teenager who will never be the same as other children. Once a mother of one such child said something that will remain forever in my heart and memory: "We are saved through our child." For this mother and father the world has not disappeared, the light has not been extinguished, but a special light glows in their souls that illumines their lives and fills them with great meaning. Such people find happiness, peace, and tranquility, but, most importantly, as St John Chrysostom says, they enter the kingdom of heaven.

We must learn how to bear our cross. It is easy to do if we link the bearing of our cross to our happiness. If in carrying our cross we become stronger, wiser, and more mature; if in carrying our cross we value each day which God gives us; if we begin to see other people in a different way, perceiving a kind look or word differently; if the bearing of our cross helps us to see the depths of the soul of another person, then we grow in strength and meaning as we draw near to the kingdom of God.

—*Homily on the Third Sunday of Lent* (April 3, 2016)

Fourth Sunday of Lent: St John Climacus

346 We are absolutely free. Yet to start ascending the steps of the ladder St John Climacus wrote about, we must hear God's calling and God's voice. This is the first step, and what is the second? As St John teaches us, it is to take a sober view of ourselves. We live inside myths about ourselves and always overestimate our importance. Our own self is essential for us. As we raise our self-esteem too high, we often come into conflict with those who do not share our high opinion of ourselves.

Correct self-appraisal helps people realize their own weaknesses and sins, so that they might say, "This and that is bad in me. I feel pangs of conscience when I treat my relatives, my friends, and my colleagues badly. I am doing things that are wrong and I have to dig deeply to find out why." These people, aware of who they really are, offer to the Lord their repentance for their wrongdoings and for their sinful thoughts and intentions.

—*Sermon on the Fourth Sunday of Lent* (April 10, 2016)

Fifth Sunday of Lent: St Mary of Egypt

347 The outstanding nineteenth century preacher Archbishop Innokenty of Korsun, when reflecting on the life of St Mary of Egypt, said that it was difficult for a man of his time to comprehend her labors, and impossible to imitate them. Yet the story of St Mary helped Archbishop Innokenty express a remarkable thought: that it is essential for man to feel in his soul the need to withdraw into the inner wilderness.

I believe that these words can also be understood by people of our twenty-first century. St Mary's path led, through repentance, from the very abyss of sin to solitude and absolute restraint of her needs and a life lived in accordance with God's will, in complete trust in God. Were she destined to die of hunger or thirst or to be torn to pieces by wild animals, she was prepared to accept it. This woman feared nothing. She sought solitude, but why? She knew that when we are alone, we understand ourselves better and see our infirmities more clearly. In our solitude, nothing from outside of us provokes us to lie or to sin. We remain alone with God. Solitude is essential for us to develop and understand our personalities.

It is unlikely, of course, that someone today would be ready to repeat the feat of St Mary of Egypt. . . . Yet it does not mean that we should disregard the story of her life in the desert. On the contrary, it means that we should pause to think. Why would this woman, so deeply entangled in the sins of the world, choose solitude? There is only one answer: when we begin to analyze our inner life seriously, when we confess our sins before God, when we become aware of our imperfections, then we feel the need to concentrate, and solitude becomes vital and necessary. Without it, the vanity of this world will give us no opportunity to do the hard work of transforming our soul.

—*Homily on the Fifth Sunday of Lent* (March 29, 2015)

Lazarus Saturday

348 When we say that by his resurrection Christ abolished death, it is not a figure of speech or an image, although these words run counter to our experience. People died before Christ's coming and still die after his resurrection. . . . However, what we call death, that is, when the human body stops functioning and decays, is not the end of life, as is clearly evidenced by the raising of Lazarus.

When by the Savior's order they were taking away the stone from Lazarus' cave, someone said: "Do not do it, he has been dead for four days, there is a stench already!" His human body had started to decompose and yet the Lord called Lazarus and he, bound head and foot in grave clothes, came out alive! The image of Lazarus, raised from the dead by God's power, helps us understand why we say that Christ destroyed death. God has power and the ability to preserve life even after the human heart stops beating and the flesh starts to decay.

—*Homily at Paschal Great Vespers* (May 1, 2016)

Palm Sunday

349 Today we heard a reading from Paul's Epistle to the Philippians, in which he says: "Rejoice in the Lord always. Again I will say, rejoice" (Phil 4.4). The text invites us to rejoice, but not as the residents of Jerusalem did in ancient times when they were meeting the Lord. How, then, should we rejoice? In the same letter the apostle also says this: "The peace of God, which surpasses all understanding, will guard your hearts and minds through Christ Jesus" (Phil 4.7).

Christ is the source of joy. He is the source of true gladness, which continues into eternal life. There is no such source outside Christ. That is why the apostle says: Always rejoice. For if you live with Christ and if Christ's peace becomes yours, then joy enters your life and becomes your greatest merit. This joy also indicates that you live a full life, independent of external circumstances.

The peace of Christ, in its turn, reveals itself in our beliefs ("minds," as the apostle puts it) and the state of our souls (so the apostle talks about "hearts") as well as in our human will directed to good deeds. St Andrew of Crete, reflecting on today's feast, said this: "Present your virtues to the Lord instead of these tree branches." There is no need to wave branches; there is no need to aspire to express external, superficial, fleeting joy. Instead, when we present to him our good deeds, open to him our hearts, and turn to him in our minds, the peace of Christ, which surpasses any peace, will guard our hearts and our minds in Christ Jesus our Lord.

—*Homily on the feast of the Entry of the Lord into Jerusalem*
(April 17, 2011)

Great and Holy Monday

350 The lives of different people bear unique fruit. Some fruit can only be seen by our families, while other people have gifts enjoyed by many. Some invent useful tools, offer new insights, or create remarkable works of art. God grants amazing talents to some people for the sake of guiding others.

However, when condemning the fig tree and the vinedressers, the Lord was referring to another kind of fruit, the fruits of the spirit. Each of us is to grow a fruit in the depth of our soul and yield it. If we come to the Last Judgment without these fruits, we will be condemned and cursed like the barren fig tree.

Perhaps the words said by the Lord to that fig tree for the edification of many people will help us on this first day of Holy Week. Without the fruit of the spirit there is no life, earthly or eternal. We know what this fruit is; St Paul teaches us about it, and the Church preaches every day about spiritual gifts (1 Cor 14.1). Holy Week is given to us so that we, having completed the pilgrimage of Lent and perhaps having failed to produce good fruit, can yet repent. We can still urge ourselves to bear fruit for the Lord, the fruit of our life that will justify us at God's Last Judgment.

—*Homily on Great and Holy Monday* (April 18, 2011)

Great and Holy Tuesday

351 The words that the Savior said about the Last Judgment before his crucifixion are his last will and testament for all of us, and we must always bear these words in mind. We must never forget about the coming judgment and our eternal destiny. As the great Russian writer Fyodor Dostoyevsky wrote, if there is no God, everything is permitted, and if there is no fear of God, man becomes a beast.

If we do not forget about judgment and eternity, then at the turning points of our life, when we are to choose whether to sin or not, this remembrance will surely help us to choose wisely. We will realize that our earthly life is nothing but an instant, that eternity lies ahead, and that the Lord invites us to enter it not as his slaves, but as his sons and daughters. He lets us follow the thorny and narrow path of our lives so that we might come "unto the measure of the stature of the fullness of Christ" (Eph 4.13), find spiritual strength, and appear worthy before him on the Day of Judgment.

—*Homily on Great and Holy Tuesday* (April 6, 2004)

Great and Holy Wednesday

352 Today's gospel reading teaches us what it means to be a Christian. To buy the precious myrrh, the sinful woman must have spent everything she had, because she was ready to offer everything to God. Perhaps she had a presentiment in her heart of the coming death of the Savior, the great teacher, healer, and prophet who led people and opened new horizons of life to them; thus, she wished to anoint him with precious myrrh. The story also tells us about money being used. Unlike Judas, who was enslaved by money and so committed an act of betrayal and died, the woman who anointed our Lord was willing to give him her most valuable possession.

—*Homily on Great and Holy Wednesday* (April 20, 2011)

Great and Holy Thursday

353 In the holy Eucharist through the power of the Holy Spirit there is actualized all that is connected to Christ: his birth, life, teaching, suffering, death, resurrection on the third day, his ascension into heaven, the sitting at the right hand of God the Father, and his second and glorious coming. All of this is made a part of the reality of our lives through the power of the Holy Spirit. In the Eucharist, the difference between the past, present, and future time disappears; through the power of the Holy Spirit, we come into contact with the kingdom of heaven and with divine grace and God himself. That is why the Divine Liturgy begins with this exclamation: "Blessed is the kingdom of the Father, and of the Son, and of the Holy Spirit!" It is the liturgy that leads us into this kingdom—not symbolically, not metaphorically, not figuratively, but in reality.

—*Homily on Great and Holy Thursday* (April 20, 2006)

Great and Holy Friday I

354 As St Ignatius Brianchaninov so wonderfully writes, "the perfection of Christianity lies in the perfect love of one's neighbor."[16] What does "perfect love" mean? It is a love that extends to strangers, to ill wishers, and even to enemies. It is a sacrificial love that transcends all human reasoning, as it cannot be contained by the framework of everyday worldly logic. We can attain it only through great spiritual endeavors that evoke the grace of God, which grants us the chance to respond to hatred with love and to evil with virtue.

—*Paschal Message* (May 1, 2016)

---

[16]St Ignatius Brianchaninov, "True Love for One's Neighbour is Based on Faith in God." An English translation is available online: "True Love for One's Neighbour Is Based on Faith in God," *Pravmir.* <http://www.pravmir.com/st-ignatius-brianchaninov-true-love-for-one-s-neighbour-is-based-on-faith-in-god/>, September 19, 2016.—*Ed.*

Great and Holy Friday II

355 It is precisely this love that Christ manifested to us when he endured terrible humiliation, suffering on the cross, and an agonizing death for our salvation. By his all-conquering love, which fills all things, hades was destroyed to its foundations, and finally the gates of paradise were opened to all humanity. In all of life's circumstances we are called upon to remember that the powers of evil are indeed illusory and not so great, for they stand no comparison with the powers of love and virtue, whose sole fount is God. Let us recall, too, that the best response to and the most effective means of resisting sin and falsehood is our sincere prayer that is lifted up from the depths of our heart: first of all, prayer that is communal, offered up in church in worship, and even more so communion of the body and blood of the Savior in the mystery of the Eucharist.

—*Paschal Message* (May 1, 2016)

Great and Holy Saturday

356 The Lord is in the tomb; yet by his divine power he descends into hell. It is not for us to understand what it means, because hell and the afterlife are beyond our human experience. . . . We do not know what occurred on Holy Saturday. We only know that what God faced was not some limited human malice, but mighty evil, and that he saved the righteous from its power. It only remains for us to thank God that it all happened through his Son, our beloved Lord Jesus Christ. And we give thanks to the Lord, celebrating tonight his resurrection—truly the victory point not only in the gospel story, but in the history of all mankind as well.

—*Homily on Great and Holy Saturday* (April 11, 2015)

Pascha I: *"The victory that God has granted to us"*

357 From year to year the good news of the resurrection resounds victoriously, encouraging us to render praise to God the Savior, who has trampled down death by death and has made us co-participants in life eternal which is to come. As we celebrate this "Feast of Feasts and Triumph of Triumphs," it is with a special spiritual feeling that we recall the redemptive act of the Savior of the world, his sufferings on the cross, and his bright resurrection. Pascha is not some beautiful legend, not some theoretical theology, and not a nod toward a popular custom established in the distant past. It is the essence and core of Christianity. It is the victory that God has granted to us.

From the time of the apostles and up to the present, the Church has preached Christ's resurrection as the greatest miracle in the history of humanity. She speaks of this miracle not only as a fact from the Gospels, but more importantly, even, as a moment of destiny for all those who have received the paschal good news. This feast bears the most direct relationship to us; for Christ's resurrection, the Lord's redemption of the fallen world, is the greatest joy that the human person can experience. No matter how difficult our life is, no matter what everyday troubles besiege us, no matter what grief and imperfections we have to endure from the world around us—all of this is nothing in comparison to the spiritual joy and hope of eternal salvation that God gives us.

—*Paschal Message* (April 19, 2014)

Pascha II: *"Unconquerable Hope"*

358 What does it mean to celebrate Pascha in a world weighed down by pain and suffering, exhausted from war and conflict, replete with hatred and enmity? What does it mean to sing that "trampling down death by death and upon those in the tombs" he has given life, when death remains the evident culmination of the earthly life of each one of us? Undoubtedly, Pascha does not abolish the real presence of death in the cosmos, but now human pain and the tragedy of our earthly life are surmounted by the resurrection of the Lord Jesus, who has granted to us, his disciples and followers, unconquerable hope in attainment of eternal life. Death is henceforth for us Christians no longer a parting, but the joyful encounter and longed for reunification with God.

—*Paschal Message* (May 1, 2016)

Pascha III: "Our Freedom"

359 For me, Pascha is the day when we celebrate our freedom. I will explain why. Sin involves the enslavement of a person. The devil seeks to enslave people and to deprive them of freedom. To do this, it is not at all necessary to put people into iron chains. To do this, the devil just needs to suggest to you that freedom is something contrary to real freedom. For instance: liberate your instincts, liberate your needs, remove all taboos, and you will be free! Yet as soon as you do this, you become a slave of your passions and a slave of the devil. That is why the resurrection of Christ is the greatest feast of victory, giving us hope for true freedom.

—*Interview on Pascha for the TV channel* Russia-1 (April 15, 2012)

Pascha IV: "There is nothing fearful in this world because we are immortal"

360 Today there are many fears in the world. Living at a higher standard of living, people begin to develop a phobia of death. These are mostly wealthy people accustomed to enjoying life, and for them, death is the ruin of everything. At death, what are their millions and billions, which give so many opportunities for pleasure? What if they are suddenly ashes and nothingness? And so they cling to life as much as they can. . . .

Christ takes away our fear of death. He tells us that there is no death, only immortality. He introduces us to this immortality that is filled with his life and his divine presence. What then does it mean for us who live in flesh in this finite world, and to an extent are always on the threshold of our physical death? Some are separated from this death by dozens of years, but even for a young person, is this a long time in the face of human history, let alone eternity? And others are separated from death by only a few years.

We live on the threshold of this event, but the resurrection of Christ fills our glimpse into the future with a great optimism and vital power. For us, there is nothing fearful in this world, because we are immortal. Nothing can be dreadful for us, because there can be no horrors for those who are aware of their immortality. Christ has announced this glorious news through his resurrection and made eternal life with God available to the entire human race.

Therefore, Christianity is a faith filled with a tremendous global optimism. We should not lose heart, have fears, or be faint-hearted. We should be afraid of nothing in this life, just as our martyrs and confessors were not afraid, just as the earliest martyrs of the Church of Christ were not afraid, just as the saints who live in the face of God are not afraid. And for this reason, the celebration of Holy Pascha helps us to be strengthened in our faith in immortality, which the Lord has given to each of us by his resurrection.

—*Homily at Paschal Great Vespers* (May 1, 2016)

Sunday of the Myrrhbearing Women

361 Today we give praises to the myrrhbearing women for their selfless ministry and for the feats of their lives, equal to that of the apostles. These praises help many of us realize the importance of women's work in our society; for, apart from necessary housework, they are burdened with great responsibility, performing numerous tasks and remaining, in a way, the pillars of their families and of the entire nation as well.

Women are, first and foremost, pillars of spiritual strength. It was the myrrh-bearing women who did not forsake Christ during the persecutions in our country. They did not abandon those successors of the apostles who ascended their Golgotha; they themselves ascended it, striving to preserve the faith in their children and grandchildren and to pass it on to succeeding generations. Our grandmothers and mothers performed a great and saving deed when they showed no fear of persecutors and served the Lord until their last breath.

—*Homily on the Third Sunday after Pascha* (May 3, 2009)

Sunday of the Blind Man

362 Can we imagine to ourselves even the most outstanding person—be he a great philosopher, political figure, emperor, or conqueror—who would say: "I am the light of the world?" Even a person beset by pride would never say this, while Christ humbly said: "I am the light of the world," as he healed the man blind from birth. And between his testimony that he is the light of the world and the fact that he heals the man, there is a deep link. The blind man in this story is a symbol of perishing humanity: he cannot see the light, he cannot distinguish objects, he cannot see the path, and he can easily go astray and become lost; he needs a guide, he needs light. . . .

In this sense, the image of the blind man is an image of the human race. We can all be blind while enjoying perfect physical sight. If we do not have the divine light in our lives, we can easily go astray. As people, we are easily influenced through the power of others' convictions, the power of propaganda, the whims of public tastes, the currents of fashions, and mere political will. We easily change the trajectory of our lives under the influence of external circumstances. And tomorrow there may arise new circumstances, and thus new changes. . . .

We live in a world where we are surrounded by thousands of false beacons, sources of light that are not from God. The Lord says to us: "I am the light of the world," and no more. Evidence is not needed; he had only just healed the man blind from birth. The Lord revealed through this miracle his testimony that only he is the light, and this means that we have to follow *this* light, no matter how many flames we encounter upon life's path that may distract us from it.

—*Homily on the Sunday of the Blind Man* (June 5, 2016)

Ascension I: *"a visible manifestation of the Savior's glory"*

363 The ascension of the Lord was of special importance in the following respect. In the Lord's life, there was no human glory. Only once, when Jesus was coming to Jerusalem to suffer, the people who had been impressed by the resurrection of Lazarus met him as a champion, spreading their clothes on the road and shouting: "Hosanna to the Son of David!" (Mt 21.8–9) However, that was vain and human glory, so the Lord did not accept their worship. Nor did he participate in that human exaltation, because he knew that the exalted sentiment of the people would soon pass away, and those who had earlier glorified him would, in a few days, demand that Pilate execute him.

Of course, the divine power and the glory of the risen Lord were revealed in the resurrection, but men did not see that glory, because no one was inside the tomb at the moment of the resurrection. The apostles saw only the signs of the resurrection, whereas the resurrection itself was seen by no one and remained God's mystery. . . .

But at the end of the gospel story the Savior's visible triumph and victory is revealed. All purposes were achieved: the human race was redeemed, the devil was conquered, and evil was trampled. God and man won in Jesus Christ, and the bodily ascension of the Lord became a visible manifestation of the Savior's glory and the victory achieved by God and man.

—*Homily on the feast of the Ascension of the Lord* (May 13, 2010)

Ascension II: "a great feast of Hope"

364 For us the Feast of the Ascension is a great feast of hope. First, we hope that, just as Christ ascended to heaven in the flesh, so we too will be called to appear at some moment in the new world described in the word of God as "a new heaven and a new earth" (Rev 21.1). The same human flesh purified from sin by the power of God and his grace will live in the new world that has no end.

God's mercy was first revealed to us in Jesus Christ, who redeemed our sins and transformed our flesh according to the primeval law that was the foundation of the entire cosmos and the human race. To experience God's mercy and renew our human nature, we should also walk the path of Christ. The Lord suffered, died, and was raised from the dead, and we, having his divine purified nature, should not darken it with sin or destroy it. We should develop the image of God, sealed in this nature, into the likeness of God. In this is the meaning of our life. The conclusion for us to draw from today's feast is that we should avoid sin and overcome it by the efforts of our will, by purifying our thoughts, and by participating in the holy mysteries of Christ. Our human nature has been set free in Christ from the power of the devil, but has not been set free from our own free will. We must choose!

Celebrating the great Feast of the Ascension, we fasten our thoughts on the mysterious future when "God will be all in all" (1 Cor 15.28), when a new heaven and a new earth will come, and when those who conquer sin in this earthly life and do the works of charity and truth together with the Savior will dwell in this world that is mysterious for us, which we call the heavenly kingdom.

—*Homily on the Ascension of the Lord* (June 9, 2016)

Pentecost

365 Today we glorify an event of tremendous importance, which in its significance can be compared to the creation of the world and the incarnation of the Son of God. We glorify the coming of the Holy Spirit to the world, and his entrance into the life of the Church. ... The divine and human natures were united in the person of Christ—according to the formula of the Fourth Ecumenical Council: unconfusedly, unchangeably, indivisibly, and inseparably—so the Holy Spirit dwells invariably together with the human nature of the Church, unconfused with it but not separate from it, spiritualizing its human nature.

—*Homily on the feast of Pentecost* (May 31, 2015)

All Saints (First Sunday after Pentecost)

366 Why do we celebrate the Day of All Saints on the first Sunday after Pentecost? We celebrate it as an assertion of the fact that the power of the Holy Spirit has transformed numerous souls, turning them away from sin toward sanctity and away from

darkness toward light. None of these saints was born holy. They became holy by their own inner efforts to open their souls to God's grace. It is in this synergy, the co-working of the divine and the human, that the fullness of human life and salvation is found, and all the rest is secondary. . . . With humility and in a calm voice the Church is called to bear witness to this: where the Holy Spirit is, there is life, and where there is no Holy Spirit, there is death. The feast of All Saints is a testimony to this. Remembering holy men of God who have shown forth in the universal Church in all times and in all nations, we bow before their vital feats, testifying that they were temples of the Holy Spirit, even as the Lord himself testified through the words of the apostle (cf. 1 Cor 6.19).

—*Homily on the Sunday of All Saints* (June 19, 2011)

Sources Used

This book is made up of selected excerpts from homilies, speeches, presentations, books, and interviews by Patriarch Kirill of Moscow and all Russia. Many of the texts have been repeatedly published in Russian, but only a few of them exist in English translation.

Most of the sayings are taken from the patriarch's homilies, which are available on the websites of the Moscow Patriarchate[1] and the Department for External Church Relations.[2] On these websites the reader will also find the Russian originals of various official statements and some of the patriarch's scholarly articles.

Patriarch Kirill's early homilies, mostly those delivered by the mid-2000s, are taken from his published collected works[3] and the printed edition of his Lenten homilies.[4] Excerpts were also taken from *A Pastor's Word*,[5] a book based on the TV show of the same name that His Holiness hosted in the 1990s. Another printed source is *The Patriarch and the Youth: Talks without Diplomacy*, published by St Daniel Monastery.[6]

[1]The Russian Orthodox Church. Official website of the Moscow Patriarchate. ‹http://www.patriarchia.ru›.

[2]The Russian Orthodox Church. Department of External Church Relations. ‹http:///www.mospat.ru›.

[3]Pat. Kirill, *Collected works, Vol. 1: A Pastor's Word Series (1991–2011)* (Moscow: Publishing House of the Moscow Patriarchate, 2014). Pat. Kirill, *Collected works, Vol. 2: A Pastor's Word (1991–2011)* (Moscow: Publishing House of the Moscow Patriarchate, 2014).

[4]Pat. Kirill, *The Mystery of Repentance: Lenten Homilies* (Moscow: Publishing House of the Moscow Patriarchate, 2012).

[5]Met. Kirill of Smolensk and Kaliningrad, *A Pastor's Word*. 3rd ed. (Moscow: DECR, 2008).

[6]*The Patriarch and the Youth: Talks without Diplomacy* (Moscow: St Daniel Monastery, 2009).

The journal *Church and Time*, published by the DECR, is another important source. Each issue of the journal contains at least one piece by the patriarch. This was the source for his speeches at the World Russian People's Council, and his speeches and presentations given at different conferences and forums on inter-Christian and inter-Orthodox relations, and on church social and political issues. All the issues used are available online on the DECR website.

Patriarch Kirill's articles and interviews for church and secular mass media are also extensively cited in this book. In particular, excerpts were taken from articles and interviews in the Orthodox magazine *Foma*,[7] the website *Radonezh.ru*,[8] the TV channels *Russia-1*,[9] *Russia-24*,[10] and *Russia Today*,[11] as well as the

[7] Pat. Kirill, "Spiritual Life is no hobby for which we may or may not have enough time," *Foma* (May 6, 2013). ‹http://foma.ru/patriarh-kirill-duhovnaya-jizn-eto-ne-hobbi.html›, October 10, 2016. [*An interview with the magazine* Foma.]; Pat. Kirill, "It is important to be grateful descendants," *Foma* (November 7, 2013). ‹http://foma.ru/vazhno-byit-blagodarnyimi-potomkami.html›, October 10, 2016. [*An interview with the magazine* Foma].

[8] Larina N., "Metropolitan Kirill: I have committed myself to the hands of God," *Radonezh.ru* (June 30, 2005). ‹http://radonezh.ru/analytics/mitropolit-kirill-ya-otdal-sebya-v-ruki-bozhii-natalya-larina-47790.html›, October 10, 2016.

[9] Pat. Kirill, "Interview on the TV show National Interest," *Official website of the Moscow Patriarchate* (November 21, 2009). ‹http://www.patriarchia.ru/db/text/950675.html›, October 10, 2016. [*Interview with the TV channel Russia*]; Pat. Kirill, "Interview on the first anniversary of the Enthronement," *Official website of the Moscow Patriarchate* (January 31, 2010). ‹http://www.patriarchia.ru/db/text/1058439.html›, October 10, 2016. [*Interview with the TV channel Russia-1*]; Pat. Kirill, "Interview," *Official website of the Moscow Patriarchate* (September 21, 2010). ‹http://www.patriarchia.ru/db/text/1280323.html›, October 10, 2016. [*An interview with the TV channel Russia-1*]; Pat. Kirill, "Interview on Pascha," *Official website of the Moscow Patriarchate* (April 15, 2012). ‹http://www.patriarchia.ru/db/text/2167419.html›, October 10, 2016. [*An interview with the TV channel Russia-1*]; Pat. Kirill, "Interview on Pascha," *Official website of the Moscow Patriarchate* (May 5, 2013). ‹http://www.patriarchia.ru/db/text/2950069.html›, October 10, 2016. [*Interview with the TV channel Russia-1*]; Pat. Kirill, "Interview on Nativity," *Official website*

information agencies *TASS*[12] and *Novosty*,[13] the gazettes *Trud*[14] and *Rossiyskaya Gazeta*,[15] and the magazines *Expert*[16] and *Smolensk*.[17] These publications are available online.

Finally, several selections were taken from the patriarch's TV show *A Pastor's Word*. Transcripts of the show are published on

of the Moscow Patriarchate (January 7, 2014). ⟨http://www.patriarchia.ru/db/text/3498045.html⟩, October 10, 2016. [*An interview with the TV channel Russia-1*]; Pat. Kirill, "Interview on Nativity," *Russia-1* (January 7, 2016). ⟨https://russia.tv/brand/show/brand_id/58947/⟩, October 10, 2016.

[10]Pat. Kirill, "A man without the habit of doing good is a deficient person," *Russia-24* (January 7, 2012). ⟨http://www.patriarchia.ru/db/text/1929614.html⟩, October 10, 2016. [*An interview with a journalist of the TV channel Russia-24*].

[11]Pat. Kirill, "Interview," *Russia Today* (February 16, 2016). <https://russian.rt.com/article/148812>, October 10, 2016.

[12]Pat. Kirill, "By denying divine truth we ruin the world," Russian News Agency TASS (March 10, 2015). ⟨http://tass.com/russia/781767⟩, October 10, 2016 [*An interview with the TASS journalist Mikhail Japaridze*].

[13]Pat. Kirill, "Those who look for the truth are already on the right way," *Russian Information Agency Novosty* (May 5, 2013). ⟨https://ria.ru/religion/20130505/935822111.html⟩, October 10, 2016 [*Interview with RIA Novosty*].

[14]Met. Kirill, "Russia is entering a new era," *Trud* (December 27, 2006). ⟨http://www.trud.ru/article/27–12-2006/111109_mitropolit_kirill_rossija_vstupaet_v_novuju_epoxu.html⟩, October 10, 2016.

[15]Pat. Kirill, "Truth and Hope," *Rossiyskaya Gazeta* (April 2, 2010). ⟨https://rg.ru/2010/04/02/patriarh.html⟩,; October 10, 2016; Pat. Kirill, "The Light of the Good," *Rossiyskaya Gazeta* (January 23, 2009). ⟨https://rg.ru/2009/01/23/kirill.html⟩, October 10, 2016 [*An interview with the gazette* Rossiyskaya Gazeta].

[16]Pat. Kirill, "The main miracle of St Sergius is the person of St Sergius himself," Expert (July 21, 2014). ⟨http://expert.ru/expert/2014/30/glavnoe-chudo-sergiya-radonezhskogo-on-sam/⟩, October 10, 2016 [*An interview with the magazine* Expert]; Pat. Kirill, "The Russian Church and European Culture," *Expert*. ⟨http://expert.ru/expert/2010/04/russkaya_cerkov_i_evropeiskaya_kultura/⟩, October 10, 2016 [*2010, Issue 4/690*].

[17]Met. Kirill, "I have taken my appointment to Smolensk as an important service entrusted to me by God," DECR website (November 22, 2006). ⟨https://mospat.ru/archive/2006/11/34036/⟩, October 10, 2016 [*An interview with the magazine* Smolensk, *2006, Issue 11*].

patriarchia.ru. In a few cases, we used recordings of the show, made our own transcriptions, and then translated these excerpts.

These selected sayings are being published in Russian by the Sts Cyril and Methodius Theological Institute for Post-Graduate Studies. The institute grants translation rights to St Vladimir's Orthodox Theological Seminary. The two sister schools are simultaneously publishing these two editions, to honor Patriarch Kirill on the occasion of his seventieth birthday.